# THE AUTHOR

Ronald Hamilton was born in 1909 and educated at Winchester College and at Magdalene College, Cambridge. He has been a schoolmaster for most of his civilian life, first at Bromsgrove School and then at Winchester College, where he taught history and modern languages for twenty-five years, and was a house master for eighteen. During the war years (1939-46) he served in the Intelligence Corps in Europe, the Middle East, India and Burma, reaching the rank of colonel and receiving the OBE. He married in 1958 and now lives in Gloucestershire.

Ronald Hamilton wrote *A Holiday History of France* after the successful publication of *Now I Remember: A Holiday History of England*, which was originally published by Chatto & Windus in 1964 and reissued as a Hogarth Press paperback, in an updated edition, in 1984. The Hogarth Press will also publish a paperback edition of his third book in this series, *A Holiday History of Scotland*.

By the same author

\*

# A HOLIDAY
# HISTORY
# OF FRANCE

## Ronald Hamilton

THE HOGARTH PRESS

LONDON

*Pour NICOLETTE*
*en t'émoignage*
*d'une longue et heureuse amitié*

Published in 1985 by
The Hogarth Press
40 William IV Street, London WC2N 4DF

First published in Great Britain by Chatto & Windus 1971
Hogarth edition offset, with additions, from original Chatto edition
Copyright © Ronald Hamilton 1971, 1985

British Library
Cataloguing in Publication Data

Hamilton, Ronald
A holiday history of France.
I. France—History
I. Title
944 DC38

ISBN 0-7012-1007-9

Printed in Great Britain by
Ebenezer Baylis & Son Ltd.,
The Trinity Press, Worcester, and London

# *Contents*

# THE OBJECT

"They order this matter better in France" – how many of us have felt that as we took our *blanc cassis* or, in more dashing mood, our *Pernod*, after a morning pottering round the cathedral or the château. This great country, by reason of its *Grand Siècle*, its Revolution and its Empire, is, in a way, shared by other nations on both sides of the Atlantic. To many of us Paris is the Queen of Cities, many of us have had the inexplicable experience of *feeling ourselves* in France, just a little bit more than we do at home. Yet our visits are not without frustrations – linguistic for some, historical for many.

It is with the latter that I am concerned. Is Hugh Capet a shadowy figure to you? Are you sound on Louis IX and Louis XI? Could you write short notes on Diane de Poitiers, Gabrielle d'Estrées, Madame de Montespan and Madame du Barry? Perhaps your holiday would be happier if, as you saw the sights, you comprehended rather more of the historical background. It is in the belief (based on bitter experience) that such is the case, that this little book has been written. In it you will find the basic facts, grouped under architectural periods – thus you can relate what you see to historical events. If it finds its place in your rucksack or car, if it lies on the table between your *Guide Michelin* and a refreshing carafe, if it answers some of the children's questions and makes your French holiday more relaxed and enjoyable, then it will have fulfilled its purpose.

R.H.

# NORTHERN FRANCE

*Showing principal places mentioned in the text*

0 20 40 60 80 100 km.

C

Boulog

PONTHIE

Cherbourg

Arque

Le Havre ■ Harfleur Roue

Bayeux ■ ■ Caen *R. Seine*

NORMANDY

Ivr

Falaise

Dreux ■

Brest

Tinchebrai

Chartres

BRITTANY

Rennes

MAINE

Blois

ANJOU

Amboise C

Tours ■ Ch

Nantes Fontevrault ■ ■ TOURA

Chinon Loches B

Ile d'Yeu

POITOU

Poitiers

La Rochelle

AQUITAINE

L

R. Gironde

Angoulême ■

Châlus

Bergerac R. Do

MAINE

ANJOU

Blois

Amboise ■ Ch

Tours ■ ■ Cher

Nantes ■ Fontevrault ■ TOURAI

Chinon Loches BE

Ile d'Yeu

POITOU

Poitiers ■

La Rochelle ■

AQUITAINE

■ Li

R. Gironde

Angoulême ■

Châlus ■

Bergerac

R. Dor

Bordeaux ■

GUYENNE

R. Garonne

Monta ■

GASCONY

Biarritz ■ ■ Bayonne

■ T

NAVARRE

Ca

Foix ■

0  20  40  60  80  100 km.

# SOUTHERN FRANCE

Showing principal places mentioned in the text

# Acknowledgments

The sources of the photographic illustrations in this book are all acknowledged individually, and I am grateful to those who have given me permission to reproduce them.

The line drawings illustrating a typical dress of each reign or republic are the work of Miss M. T. Ritchie, who prepared them specially for this volume.

I wish to express my thanks for being allowed to quote from the following:

*A History of France* by G. W. Kitchin, D.D. (Clarendon Press, Oxford).

*A History of Europe* by H. A. L. Fisher (Eyre and Spottiswoode).

*The Capetian Kings of France* by Robert Fawtier, translated by Lionel Butler and R. J. Adam (Macmillan and Co Ltd.).

*Citizen King* by T. E. B. Howarth (Eyre and Spottiswoode).

Article in *The Daily Telegraph* by J. B. Firth.

I have, on occasion, been able to check points, only partially explained elsewhere, from Dr Gaston Sirjean's "Encyclopédie Généalogique des Maisons Souveraines du Monde – Les Capétiens Directs, Les Valois, Les Bourbons".

I have received much encouragement and practical assistance from friends: Marion Coate, M.B.E., Chevalier de la Légion d'Honneur, Chevalier de l'Ordre des Palmes Académiques, Secretary of the Franco-British Society; Valerie Gaunt, Chevalier de l'Ordre National du Mérite, Council Member of the Alliance Française; Basil Robinson of the Victoria and Albert Museum, Robert Cecil of the Wallace Collection and Ruthven Hall of Winchester College.

In France my way was smoothed by Mademoiselle Nicolette Boillot, to whom this book is dedicated. I wish, further, to express my thanks to Monsieur Adhémar, of the Bibliothèque Nationale; to Monsieur Mahieu of the Archives Nationales; to Prince Raoul de Broglie of the Musée Condé, Chantilly, and Prince Dominique de Broglie; to Madame Tureau of the Service de Documentation Photographique des Musées Nationaux at Versailles; to Monsieur Gérard Cornet-Vernet, to whom I owe my information on French Twentieth Century architecture, and to the employees of Photographie Giraudon.

In a very special category I place Jack Blakiston, of Winchester College, my one-time secretary, Micky Bartlett, my sister, Mary Ferguson and my wife.                                                    R.H.

# ROMANESQUE
## (L'Art Roman)
## 987–1137

| | |
|---|---|
| Hugh Capet | 987–996 |
| Robert II (The Pious) | 996–1031 |
| Henry I | 1031–1060 |
| Philip I | 1060–1108 |
| Louis VI (The Fat) | 1108–1137 |

*(In England cf. NORMAN 1066–1189)*

| | |
|---|---|
| Ethelred II (The Unready) | 979–1016 |
| Edmund Ironside | 1016 |
| Canute | 1016–1035 |
| Harold I | 1035–1040 |
| Hardicanute | 1040–1042 |
| Edward the Confessor | 1042–1066 |
| Harold II | 1066 |
| William the Conqueror | 1066–1087 |
| William II (Rufus) | 1087–1100 |
| Henry I (Beauclerc) | 1100–1135 |
| Stephen | 1135–1154 |

ROMANESQUE
Abbey of Fontevrault
(French Government Tourist Office. Photographie Karquel)

# ROMANESQUE (L'Art Roman)
# 987–1137

The notes which follow avoid the difficult technicalities
of architecture but sketch, broadly, the characteristics of
the main styles. They are here in order to assist you to link
your sightseeing with the History of France.

It is, of course, impossible to lay down accurate dates for
architectural periods – but the end of the tenth century to
something like the end of the first quarter of the twelfth is
reasonably acceptable as the span covered by the style
known as "Romanesque" (*L'art roman*), though you may
well find examples of it before the coronation of Hugh Capet
and after the death of Louis VI.

In England the corresponding style is "Norman" – a
word suggesting semi-circular arches, thick walls, small
windows and fat, tough cylindrical pillars. In France, a
country neither politically nor artistically united, we find
infinite variations on this theme. Thus at least eight schools,
each displaying regional characteristics, are to be found:
in Normandy, in the North, eastward towards the Rhine,
in Burgundy, Provence, Languedoc, Auvergne and the
West. Many influences were at work. The Crusades were no
doubt responsible for the cupolas in the general area of the
Auvergne, new fashions were carried along the pilgrim
routes, the legacy of Rome lay heavy on Provence (and,
indeed, wherever there were Roman remains, e.g. in the
nave of Autun cathedral), while from the great Burgundian
abbey of Cluny there came a radiation of sophisticated
ideas in construction and design.

Ruskin preferred Romanesque architecture to that of
ancient Greece, for "building an arch, vault or dome is a
nobler and more ingenious work than laying a flat stone or
beam over the space to be covered". He also regarded it as
"healthy". It looks it.

Hugh Capet

*(Bibliothèque Nationale, Estampes, Paris)*

# HUGH CAPET, 987–996

Born ? 941, was ? 46 in 987, and ? 55 when he died.

Married Adelaide of Aquitaine and had one son:
                    ROBERT II, the Pious
and three daughters.

*Thumbnail Sketch*    A prince of undoubted courage and piety, painstaking and able in negotiation, a most determined dynast.


## WHAT TO KNOW

It was as Louis Capet that Louis XVI appeared before the National Convention in Paris on 11 December 1792 and mounted the steps of the scaffold in the following January. The name, as a royal one, went back eight hundred and five years. On 5 July 987 Hugh Capet, emerging from an anarchical welter of feudal lords, elected King of the French by his peers and supported by powerful ecclesiastics, was crowned at Noyon by Adalberon, Archbishop of Rheims. The inception of this formidable dynasty may be taken as a starting-point for the history of France.

The fair land with which we are concerned had experienced the discipline of the *Pax Romana*, the coming of Christianity, the upheaval of the Barbarian invasions, the rule of the Merovingian house, the formation and disintegration of the Carolingian Empire and finally the fissiparous development of feudalism in the West Frankish kingdom. Against this background the future of the new monarch and his heirs seemed unpromising, for, outside the royal domain, "Hugh and his first descendants were no more than the feudal lords of about sixty dukes and counts, of independent hereditary power, who disdained the control of laws and legal assemblies, and whose disregard of their sovereign was revenged by the disobedience of their inferior vassals" (Gibbon). The story, probably apocryphal, is told that when the first Capet addressed the recalcitrant lord of Périgord with the words: "Who made you Count?" he was met with the swift rejoinder: "Who made you King?"

But, in fact, Hugh Capet enjoyed certain solid advantages. His royal domain extended from a point some forty miles north-east of Paris to about twenty miles south of Orleans (an overall distance of approximately one hundred and thirty miles) and measured some fifty miles from west to east at its widest point. Paris and Orleans, lying respectively on the great rivers Seine and Loire, were natural centres of communication by water and by road, while the Isle of France, centring on Paris, was already of traditional political importance. Further to this, though no more than *primus inter pares* amongst great feudal lords, Hugh Capet was well connected. His brother Henry was Duke of Burgundy, his sister was wife to Richard the Fearless, Duke of Normandy, while he himself married Adelaide of Aquitaine. He was, also, the Lord's anointed, Abbot of Saint Denis near the Seine and of Saint Martin on the Loire. He enjoyed the firm support of Archbishop Adalberon and of his intensely able secretary Gerbert, who would eventually follow his master in the archdiocese and subsequently become Pope Silvester II.

But Hugh's path was in no way smooth. The Carolingian pretender, Charles of Lorraine, marched against him from the North, the Duke of Aquitaine menaced him from the South, Adalberon of Rheims died. In order to win an adherent amongst his opponents Hugh supported Arnulf, Charles' nephew, as the Archbishop's successor, a policy which not only offended Gerbert,

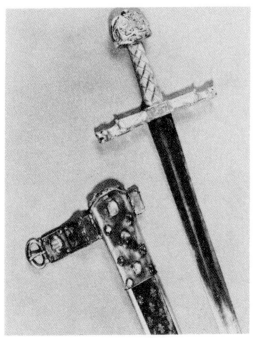

Coronation sword and scabbard of the Kings of France,
period of Charlemagne
*(Louvre, Paris. Photo des Musées Nationaux)*

the obvious choice, but failed to pay off. Eventually, however,
aided by his Norman brother-in-law and profiting by treachery in
the enemy camp, Hugh secured the persons both of Charles and
Arnulf – the latter to suffer deposition while the former perished
in prison at Orleans. The way to the archiepiscopal throne of
Rheims was now cleared for Gerbert, but these arbitrary ex-
changes incensed Pope John XV, with whom disputes raged until
the end of the reign. The exhausted monarch was carried off by
small-pox on 24 October 996, but, demonstrating the tenacious
sense of family which characterized his race, he had taken the
precaution as long ago as 30 December 987 of having his son
Robert crowned as his associate King and successor. Persistence
in this policy by the Capets was to establish the principle of
hereditary monarchy.

Robert II, by L. Gautier

*(Bibliothèque Nationale, Estampes, Paris)*

# ROBERT II (THE PIOUS), 996–1031

## (Son of HUGH CAPET and Adelaide of Aquitaine)

Born 970, was 27 when he succeeded his father, and 61 when he died.

Married Rozalle-Suzanne of Italy. No issue. Marriage dissolved.
Married Bertha of Burgundy. No issue. Marriage dissolved.
Married Constance of Arles and had four sons, including:

> HENRY I (Duke of Burgundy 1015 to 1032)
>
> Robert (Duke of Burgundy 1032 to 1076)

and one daughter:

> > Adela, who married (1)   Richard III, Duke of
> > Normandy, (2) Baldwin V, Count of Flanders.

*Thumbnail Sketch*   Pious, charitable, musical and cultivated (he always travelled with books) – Robert's sustained campaigning suggests a man of tougher fibre than is pictured by the monastic historians.

## WHAT TO KNOW

Robert the Pious was much married – first to Rozalle-Suzanne of Italy, childless and considerably his senior, from whom he parted on grounds of the age-gap between them in 992. He then wed a beloved distant cousin, Bertha of Burgundy, a union opposed by Popes John XV and Gregory V on grounds of consanguinity. The formidable weapons of excommunication and interdict brought Robert to his knees, he and Bertha parted in 1001, and two years later he married the handsome termagant Constance of Arles. She brought with her a suite of Aquitanians whose footwear, hair styles and short coats incensed the established northern clergy as much as they enchanted Robert's unsophisticated courtiers. Constance gave Robert four sons, one daughter and great unhappiness. But he now had heirs.

In common with other early Capets Robert's major preoccupation was the maintenance of good order within his own domain. In this, after the quietly determined fashion of his family, he achieved modest progress, though there were plenty of troubles. The year 1000 (when the end of the world was widely expected) brought a general malaise upon the land, there was heresy at Orleans – savagely suppressed in 1022 – and barons were continually rebellious. But, despite all this, Robert, by pertinacious campaigning (1003–1015) managed to acquire Burgundy – already the home of a blossoming culture and a civilizing monasticism radiating from Cluny – which had been left without an heir by the death of his uncle. Robert made the duchy over to his son Henry, but kept effective control of it during his own lifetime, which was one of the reasons which drove Henry and his brother Robert, supported by Queen Constance, to hostilities with their father during the concluding years of the reign. Nonetheless Henry, according to rapidly growing family tradition, was associated in the Kingship in 1027.

Burgundy had become Capetian, but there was no question of attempting the impossible task of bringing all of what we would now call France under the family's sway. Indeed as yet there were no strong forces making for unity – not even the bond of common language. Feudal sub-division seemed the natural and inevitable situation. The horrifyingly picturesque Fulk Nerra (the Black) – powerful Count of Anjou (987–1040) – led a life in which violence alternated with penitential pilgrimages to the Holy Land, on one of which he is said to have achieved a priceless relic by biting off a piece of the Holy Sepulchre. South of the Loire a vast area was ruled by William V, Duke of Aquitaine, while to the west the Norman Dukes – successively Richard II, Richard III and Robert the Devil – were princes of great power. Already in 1016 the Normans returning from Palestine had set foot in Italy. In 1027 Robert the Devil's roving eye fell upon Arlette, the tanner's daughter, with the result that William the Conqueror was born at Falaise. Robert the Pious' good relations with Aquitaine and

Sion Gospels. *c.* 1000
*(Victoria and Albert Museum. Crown Copyright)*

Normandy constituted an important factor in ensuring his
survival.

The most important thing that the early Capets could do was
to survive as Kings. To achieve this it was necessary to remain at
least as powerful as their neighbours and to exercise patience and
perseverance in cultivating the hereditary principle. So much was
being attained by Robert the Pious when he died of fever at
Melun on 20 July 1031.

Henry I, by L. Gautier

*(Bibliothèque Nationale, Estampes, Paris)*

# HENRY I, 1031–1060

(Son of ROBERT II, THE PIOUS, and Constance of Arles)
Born 1008, was 23 when he succeeded his father, and 52 when he
died.

Married Matilda, daughter of Conrad the Salic of Germany. No
issue.
Married Anna of Kiev, and had three sons, including:
> PHILIP I
> Hugh, Count of Vermandois

*Thumbnail Sketch* A man of pleasure, but courageous, who
struggled to subdue his feudal vassals, with varying success.


## WHAT TO KNOW

The reign of Henry I opened inauspiciously. Men were
troubled in mind by the thousandth anniversary of the crucifixion,
hideous famine (the seventh since 987) swept across Europe,
Constance the Queen Mother incited her favourite and younger
son Robert to rebel. With the help of Robert the Devil, Duke of
Normandy and Fulk Nerra, Count of Anjou, order was restored.
The Normans were paid by the cession of the Vexin (South-East
of Rouen) which brought their frontier within a day's march of
Paris, and the King felt it necessary to pacify his brother Robert
with the Duchy of Burgundy, which would not come back to the
French crown until 1477.

Private wars, conducted by rival nobles, provinces, towns and
villages, were the curse of the age. Ecclesiastical councils attempted to mitigate this by proclaiming "The Peace of God" – for the
protection of churches, monks, merchants, peasants, "colts, oxen,
asses, sheep, goats and pigs" – with varying success. "The Truce
of God", announced at Nice in 1041, forbad fighting from
Thursday evening to Monday morning; to these long week-ends
were eventually added Feast Days and the periods of Advent and
Lent, leaving a restricted fighting season of something under
three months in the year. In addition to this, peace-associations
were formed in every diocese. These measures, backed by the
dread sanction of excommunication, were by no means ineffective,

and did much for the increase of safety and culture.

In the early years of his reign Henry profited greatly from his alliance with Robert the Devil, of Normandy. When the latter died at Nicaea in 1035, on his way back from Palestine, leaving the Duchy to his eight-year-old bastard son William, traditional Capet policy began to undergo a change. It is true that French troops assisted the young Duke to put down a serious nobles' rebellion at Val-ès-Dunes in 1047, but Henry attempted to profit from the rivalry between William and Geoffrey Martel, Count of Anjou (1040–1060) – Fulk Nerra's successor – only to suffer two defeats at Norman hands, the first in 1054 at Mortemer, the second at Varaville four years later.

On these two occasions knights from as far afield as Flanders and Gascony rode under Henry's ill-fated banner, but the truth is that "Normandy had become, under a dynasty of vigorous Dukes, the strongest and most coherent principality in Western Europe" (H. A. L. Fisher, *A History of Europe*). The Normans had shed their Norse speech in favour of what we may call French, but retained the *wanderlust* of their ancestors. They fought the Saracens in Spain, ten of the twelve sons of Tancred of Hauteville left their

home near Coutances for military adventure in Italy, where the sixth of them – Robert "Guiscard" (the cunning) – became Duke of Apulia and Calabria (respectively the heel and toe of the country) in 1059. The conquest of England was imminent, the brilliant Norman Kingdom of Sicily was not far distant in time, and in many ways the Duke of Normandy cut a more impressive figure than the King of the French.

But the consolidation of the Capet dynasty and domain remained the major preoccupation. When Matilda, Henry's first Queen, died, he was terrified of consanguinity complications, sought a wife from

La Daurade. Cloister capital. Daniel in the Lion's Den
*(Musée des Augustins, Toulouse. Photo des Musées Nationaux)*

far away and married, in 1051, Anna, daughter of the Grand
Duke of Kiev. Their eldest son, named Philip in honour of his
mother's reputed descent from Philip of Macedon, was crowned
on Whitsunday 1059. Henry I died just over a year later, on
4 August 1060, leaving his throne to a child of seven.

XXXVIII.                         ROY.

PHILIPPE I

L'an 1095. Sous ce Regne le
Pape Urbain II. se refugia en France
et y Prescha luy même la Croisade a la So-
licitation de Pierre l'hermite Gentilhomme Picard.
Le Nombre des Croisez passa celuy de trois cent mil

Depuis 1060.      B.R.      jusqu'à 1108.

Philip I
Urban II preaches the First Crusade
*(Bibliothèque Nationale, Estampes, Paris)*

# PHILIP I, 1060–1108

## (Son of HENRY I and Anna of Kiev)

Born 1053, was 7 when he succeeded his father, and 55 when he died.

Married Bertha of Frisia (marriage dissolved 1091), and had three sons, including:

> LOUIS VI

and one daughter:

> > Constance, who married (1) Hugh of Champagne, (2) Bohemund of Hauteville, Duke of Calabria and Prince of Antioch

Married Bertrada of Montfort, and had two sons and two daughters.

*Thumbnail Sketch* Stigmatized variously by historians as "dissolute", "profligate", "apathetic" and "worthless", Philip I was, nonetheless, a painstaking, consistent and realistic consolidator of the domain.

## WHAT TO KNOW

The fact that Philip I was an infant demanded a regency, which was placed in the capable hands of Baldwin V, Count of Flanders. The latter had married the King's aunt – Adela, sister of Henry I – and their daughter Matilda was consort to William the Conqueror. The systematic travels of uncle and nephew throughout the Capet domain enforced domestic discipline, but they could not hinder the Norman Duke's descent upon England in 1066 – a triumph of planning and execution. This feat brought a menacing increase in Norman strength, though comfort might be derived, in the long run, from the fact that the actual Norman power centre moved from Caen to more distant London. Positive gain for Philip accrued from the wreck of the mighty work accomplished by Fulk Nerra and Geoffrey Martel in expanding Anjou, for the latter died heirless in 1060 and his nephews – Geoffrey the Bearded and Fulk Réchin – disputed the heritage. Similarly other great feudal states (e.g. those of Aquitaine and Eudes of Blois) had suffered from partition or war. But there was little rest for the French King. After fruitless hostilities with his vassal Robert the Frisian (son of Baldwin V) in 1071, Philip became heavily preoccupied with the continental activities of the Anglo-Normans, whose family difficulties he sensibly attempted to exploit, and whose enemies he consistently befriended. The irregularities of his private existence brought complications in their train, earning him the reproof of the great reforming Pope Gregory VII (Hildebrand) as early as 1074, and culminating about 1092 when he put away his Queen, Bertha of Frisia (William of Malmesbury blames her *embonpoint*) and carried off Fulk Réchin's attractive wife Bertrada of Montfort. Despite excommunication and interdict Bertrada charmed Philip until his death in 1108, when she withdrew to the abbey of Fontevrault.

Philip's excommunication disqualified him from obeying the summons of Peter the Hermit, endorsed by Pope Urban II at Clermont Ferrand in 1095, which precipitated the folly and gallantry of the Crusades. This astounding movement was occasioned by the conquering advance of the Seljuk Turks which menaced the Eastern Emperor at Constantinople, the Christians domiciled at Jerusalem, travellers to the Holy Places, and East–West traders. All these appealed to Western Christendom, nor did their cry go unheard. Religious revival, disciplined by the spread of

monasticism, had been at work; increased population and famine rendered the mythical milk and honey of Palestine enticing; an eastward push suited the soldierly ambitions of the Normans in Sicily and the commercial aspirations of the Italian seaboard cities; militaristic lords could acquire merit from pilgrimage, by practising blamelessly the one art they fully understood, and the Papacy hoped for an unprecedented position of command. So Peter the Hermit and Walter the Penniless led off a rabble, most of whom perished near Nicaea, to be followed later by three armies under Godfrey of Bouillon, Hugh of Vermandois – Philip I's brother – and Raymond of Toulouse. Marching by different routes they

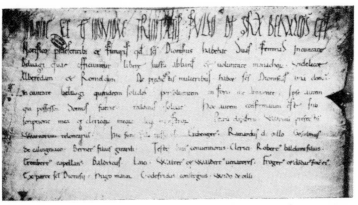

Document of Foulques, Bishop of Beauvais (1089–1095) emancipating
two serfs, property of the Abbot of Saint Denis, at Beauvais
*(Service Photographique des Archives Nationales, Paris)*

captured Jerusalem on 15 July 1099, having suffered severe losses,
but displaying at times high technical distinction. They founded
four feudal states in the Middle East: the Latin Kingdom of
Jerusalem and the principalities of Edessa, Antioch and Tripoli.

No monarch benefited more than Philip I from the absence of
great lords, for the crusading impulse was pre-eminently French.
Here was a symptom of national unity which, though owing
nothing to him, could be exploited by later Capets. Hierarchical
feudal society was shaken by these events. The movement known
as the Enfranchisement of the Communes, whereby towns,
benefiting from increased trade born of travel and war, negotiated
liberties from the great men to whom they owed obligations,
gathered momentum. Proud belfries, symbols of urban independence and power, arose. Kings and citizens sometimes allied
against nobles who, themselves, were increasing in civilization,
influenced both by ideals of chivalry, emanating from the church,
and by contact with the superior culture of their Saracen foes.
Men's minds were awakening and, by the turn of the century,
Peter Abelard was challenging William of Champeaux in the
Parisian Cathedral School of Notre Dame.

In 1100 Philip I added Bourges to his domain by pure chance
(its lord needed cash for crusading activities) and made his son
Louis joint King. There is little doubt that his reign left the
dynasty more firmly established than it had been at his accession.

Louis VI
*(Bibliothèque Nationale, Estampes, Paris)*

# LOUIS VI (THE FAT), 1108–1137
## (Son of PHILIP I and Bertha of Frisia)

Born 1081, was 27 when he succeeded his father, and 56 when he died.

Married Lucienne of Rochefort, whom he repudiated. No issue.
Married Adelaide of Maurienne and had seven sons, including:
>LOUIS VII

and one daughter:
>>Constance, who married (1) Eustace, son of Stephen of England, (2) Raymond V of Toulouse

*Thumbnail Sketch*  A gluttonous sensualist perhaps – certainly not the paragon described by Suger – but a courageous, energetic, intelligent opportunist.

## WHAT TO KNOW

Despite the absence of certain undesirable barons on crusading activities Louis VI found, even within the royal domain, that he was obstructed by overmighty subjects menacing Paris from North and South. Feudal turbulence was, of course, endemic, and from 1100 (for it was then, effectively, that he began to reign) Louis struggled against it. He enjoyed the support of the church, as represented by his friend and counsellor Suger, Abbot of Saint Denis – gay scholar, of humble origin, unostentatious ascetic, orderly administrator, one of the founders of the realm of France. Louis recruited three hundred young gallants (*damoiseaux*) as household troops, and, seeing himself as the source from which justice emanated, sought and found allies amongst the humbler folk who desired protection against noble, rebellious marauders. Appreciating that urban development militated against feudalism he encouraged or suppressed communal aspirations, as opportunity served, scattered his own representatives – provosts (*prévôts*) – about the domain, and functioned with the primitive administrative machinery of the seneschal, who directed his household, the chancellor, who aided him in matters secretarial and judicial, the butler, the chamberlain and the constable. This all boils down to vigorous and successful pursuit of traditional Capet policy.

There were, of course, germs of nationalism here, and the achievements of the French King were not entirely parochial, even if certain great vassals, from Flanders to Gascony, still tended to take a light-hearted view of their feudal obligations. The Anglo-Norman monarchy, the strongest in Europe, received an access of power when Henry I of England defeated his brother Robert, Duke of Normandy, at Tinchebrai (1106). War between Louis and Henry, in which the former supported William Clito, son of Robert, against his uncle, was intermittent from 1113 to 1135. The battle of Brenneville (1119) is remarkable in that the total losses amounted to three knights – a casualty rate presumably attributable either to the civilizing influence of chivalry or the technical progress of armourers. The year 1125 is significant in that Henry I enlisted the aid of his son-in-law Henry V, the Holy Roman (Germanic) Emperor, a step which was countered by the unusually gratifying response accorded to Louis' summons of knights from outside the domain. A formidable host gathered under the *Oriflamme* – the first occasion upon which this ancient banner of the Counts of the Vexin, green-tasselled, vermilion, and flying from a gilded staff, had been unfurled for a King of France. The Emperor withdrew. In addition to this, in 1126, Louis VI righted a wrong done by the Count of Auvergne to the Bishop of

Clermont, took hideous revenge (1127) on the murderers of Charles the Good, Count of Flanders, and, in 1131, supported Pope Innocent II, who had taken refuge in France, against the anti-pope Anacletus II, on the advice of Saint Bernard of Clairvaux.

This young noble, who joined the Cistercians at Cîteaux in 1113 and founded the abbey of Clairvaux in 1115, was a dominant church figure by 1130. His final triumph over the more attractive Peter Abelard, *clarus doctor* of the Paris schools and lover of Héloïse, was yet to come, but their dispute bears witness to the intellectual ferment of the age. For against a background of castles and romanesque churches the *Chansons de Geste*

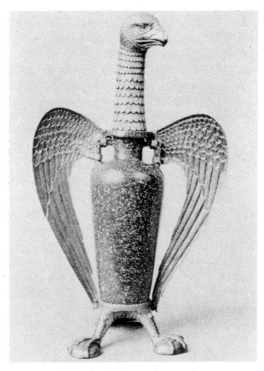

Vase in the form of an eagle

*( Treasury of Abbey of St. Denis. Louvre, Paris. Photo des Musées Nationaux)*

(the *Chanson de Roland* dates from the early twelfth century) were being rendered by *jongleurs*, while at Ste-Geneviève, Notre Dame de Paris and Nogent-sur-Seine, scholars were wrangling over Aristotelian logic.

Two strokes of luck concluded the reign. England's Henry I died in 1135, precipitating the anarchical period of dispute between his heiress Matilda, widow of the Emperor Henry V and now wife of Geoffrey of Anjou, and his nephew Stephen, which greatly weakened the Anglo-Norman power. And, in 1137, it was possible for Louis to marry his son (associate King since 1131) to Eleanor of Aquitaine, whose marriage portion brought lands stretching from the Loire to the Pyrenees. When Louis the Fat died on 1 August 1137 he had deserved well of his family.

# EARLY GOTHIC
## (L'Art Gothique Primitif)
### 1137–1226

| Louis VII (The Young) | 1137–1180 |
| Philip II (Augustus) | 1180–1223 |
| Louis VIII | 1223–1226 |

*(In England cf. EARLY ENGLISH 1189–1307)*

| Stephen | 1135–1154 |
| Henry II | 1154–1189 |
| Richard I (Coeur de Lion) | 1189–1199 |
| John (Lackland) | 1199–1216 |
| Henry III | 1216–1272 |

Exterior of Laon Cathedral

# EARLY GOTHIC
## (L'Art Gothique Primitif)
### 1137–1226

William Morris, visiting Louviers in 1855, wrote: "I have never, either before or since, been so much struck with the difference between the early and late Gothic, and by the greater nobleness of the former."

You will decide for yourself – but you can hardly fail to be impressed as you stand before the West front of a great church of this period, gazing at three heavily ornamented doors, at windows either "rose" or with sharp "lancet" points, and, as you walk around, you will observe flying buttresses bearing witness to an advanced comprehension of stresses. And, as you penetrate within, you will realize that Gothic differs from Romanesque above all by the use of the pointed arch – it is, in fact, ogival architecture. (Note that the word "*ogival*", in French, simply means "pointed" or "Gothic", and does not imply the arch which we call "ogee" – see page 93.) The pointed arch, obviously invented again and again in different places, solved the vital problem, inherent in semi-circular vaulting, of how to build a stone roof over an oblong compartment without the awkwardness of having arches of varying heights: it thus assured the general use of stone rather than timber in roof construction, thereby minimizing the risk of fire which many Romanesque churches had suffered.

It may help you if you bear in mind the dates of the following cathedrals: Sens (1130–1170), Saint-Denis (1132–1144), Noyon (1132–1186), Notre Dame de Paris (1160–1245), Laon (1174–1233), and Chartres, restarted after a fire (1194–1233). There is, of course, overlapping with the previous and the subsequent period – but take 1144, the consecration of Saint-Denis, as a key date. There is reason to believe that the representative congregation of notables assembled on that occasion carried the new ideas far and wide in France.

Louis VII, Engraving by Pannier, after Decaisne

*(Bibliothèque Nationale, Estampes, Paris)*

# LOUIS VII (THE YOUNG), 1137–1180
(Son of LOUIS VI and Adelaide of Maurienne)

Born 1120, was 17 when he succeeded his father, and 59 when he died.

Married Eleanor of Aquitaine and had two daughters:

> Mary, who married Henry, Count of Champagne
> Alix, who married Theobald, Count of Blois

Married Constance of Castile and had two daughters, including:

> Margaret, who married (1) Henry, second son of Henry II of England; (2) Bela III, King of Hungary

Married Adela of Champagne and had one son:

> PHILIP II (Augustus)

and two daughters – of whom Agnes married, successively, two Eastern Emperors: Alexius II and Andronicus I

*Thumbnail Sketch*   A chivalrous, bookish churchman who, in fact, lacked neither realism nor courage.

## WHAT TO KNOW

The Stephen-Matilda rivalry for the English crown meant hostilities on both sides of the Channel, and even though Matilda's husband – Geoffrey Plantagenet, Count of Anjou – laboriously reduced Normandy and became its Duke, there could be no serious Anglo-Norman menace in the early days of Louis VII. That lovely, but perhaps over-spirited heiress, his Queen, favoured what turned out to be an abortive attempt to reduce one of her old enemies, the Count of Toulouse (1141) and in the same year the King became involved, with Suger's support, in a dispute with Pope Innocent II over the royal right to name a new Archbishop for Bourges. Theobald, Count of Champagne (whose sons – Henry and Theobald – would later marry into the Royal family, see above) took the Papal side, and Louis marched against him. The pious monarch now placed an intolerable burden on his conscience by burning the church of the Marne town of Vitry-en-Perthois (long known as Vitry-le-Brûlé), in which some 1,300 refugees perished. Peace with the Pope could scarcely be achieved without penance, and the obvious answer was to take the cross. Saint Bernard, who had by now triumphed over Abelard and was going from strength to strength, preached with tremendous effect at Vézelay (1146) and so off went Conrad III of Germany and Louis VII of France to waste their incompatible armies on the disastrous Second Crusade (1147–49). Suger won the title *Pater Patriae* for his brilliant government during the King's absence – and learnt with alarm that the *malaise* existing between Louis and Queen Eleanor had reached breaking point at Antioch, where there had been malicious references to her relationship with an uncle. But Suger died in 1151 and in 1152 the Council of Beaugency found grounds for divorce (consanguinity!) which permitted Eleanor, after a lapse of two months, to put her un-doubted charms and vast lands at the disposal of Henry Plan-tagenet, son of Matilda and Geoffrey, who was already Count of Anjou, Count of Maine and Duke of Normandy. Louis, concerned – like the rest of his dynasty – with having a male heir, had certainly not calculated upon this!

Opinions are divided as to whether the divorce, with its accom-panying territorial loss, represents an egregious error of statesman-ship on the part of Louis VII, or whether, in fact, Aquitaine was too great a fief for the contemporary monarchy to absorb. It was followed, in 1154, by Henry Plantagenet's acces-sion as Henry II of England, thus creating what is known as the Angevin Empire, the Continen-tal dominions of which extended from the Channel to the Pyrenees. Surveying, in con-trast, his own domain Louis VII observed: "in France we have only bread, wine and gaiety", and made it his policy to embar-rass this portentous vassal whenever op-portunity presented itself. His position as suzerain had its advantages as when, in 1159, Louis assisted the Count of Toulouse and, by his mere presence in that city, prevented Henry II besieging it. And the devout Louis made astute use of ecclesiastical support not only against his Angevin but also against his

Chalice of Abbot Suger, from Saint-Denis.
*(National Gallery of Art, Washington D.C. Widener Collection)*

Germanic rival; did not Pope Alexander III, energetic and suc-
cessful opponent of Henry II and the Emperor Frederick
Barbarossa, take refuge in France when anti-popes were raised up
against him? And did not Louis receive Henry's recalcitrant
Archbishop Becket with honour? There were also quarrels between
Henry and his sons, and differences between Henry and his Queen
– Louis' ex-wife – which could be exploited. Nevertheless, despite
all efforts, this curtain-raiser to the Hundred Years War left
Henry II the most powerful monarch in Europe with a firm grip
on his possessions.

But progress had been made. In 1165 Louis' third wife had
borne him a son, the celebrated Philip Augustus, at whose coronation at Rheims in 1179 it is said that the "Twelve Peers of France"
(the Dukes of Normandy, Burgundy and Guyenne; the Counts of
Champagne, Flanders and Toulouse; the Archbishop of Rheims;
the Bishops of Laon, Noyon, Châlons, Beauvais and Langres)
assisted. The reign witnessed advances both in urban and rural
civilization and it is noteworthy that Paris was becoming increasingly popular with members of the Capet family – perhaps
because of the abundance of game in its vicinity.

On 11 September 1180, stricken with paralysis in the previous
year while returning from pilgrimage to the shrine of Saint
Thomas of Canterbury, Louis VII died.

Philip II
*(Bibliothèque Nationale, Estampes, Paris)*

# PHILIP II (AUGUSTUS), 1180–1223

## (Son of LOUIS VII and Adela of Champagne)

Born 1165, was 15 when he succeeded his father, and 57 when he died.

Married Isabella of Hainault and had one surviving son:
## LOUIS VIII
Married Ingeborg of Denmark, whom he immediately repudiated, but re-acknowledged after the death of Agnes of Meran.
Married, irregularly, Agnes of Meran and had one daughter and one son.

*Thumbnail Sketch*  Beneath a bucolic exterior this formidably realist monarch hid a clear understanding of policy, and of war. Patiently, sagaciously – and eminently successfully – he practised the art of the possible.

## WHAT TO KNOW

It is reported that the young Philip II observed: "I desire that at the end of my reign the monarchy will be as powerful as in the time of Charlemagne." To achieve this object it was necessary to obtain real mastery over his own feudatories and to break up the Angevin Empire.

The northern nobility, alarmed at the King's acquisition of Artois through his marriage with Isabella of Hainault, made trouble at once, and some five years were spent in dealing with the rebellious rulers of Flanders and Burgundy and their associates. By 1186 Philip emerged triumphant, with Amiens and the Vermandois added to his possessions.

The ruler of the Angevin Empire, England's Henry II, with whom he had already on occasion conferred under the oak of Gisors, now claimed Philip's attention. Befriending the great Plantagenet's perfidious sons – Richard Coeur de Lion and John Lackland – he had the satisfaction of knowing, by 1189, that his rival, exhausted and saddened by family treachery, lay in his tomb at Fontevrault.

Coeur de Lion, now Richard I of England, had been Philip's intimate friend – the companion of his board and, incongruously,

his bed. Together these two young men responded to the call of
the Third Crusade, occasioned by the brilliant Saladin's recapture
of Jerusalem in 1187, and set out from Vézelay in 1190. The strain
of campaigning induced frequent quarrels, culminating at Acre,
where Philip left Richard, enthusiastically involved in military
activities, convinced that he, personally, could be more profitably
employed in Europe. Once home he intrigued with John Lackland
against Richard, invaded Normandy, despite fair promises made
in Palestine, and did all he could to prolong the English King's
celebrated imprisonment in Germany – a disaster which befell
him as he returned from the wars. In 1194 Coeur de Lion re-
appeared – liberated and vengeful – and the tide of battle swept
to and fro. The brilliantly conceived Château Gaillard arose,
blocking Philip's road to Rouen, and desultory hostilities continued until 1199, when the crossbowman Pierre Basile did signal
service to the Capet monarchy by picking off Richard before
Châlus.

Consistency now demanded the discomfiture of Richard's
successor John. Here Arthur of Brittany, twelve-year-old posthumous son of John's elder brother Geoffrey, could be utilized,
since a number of Angevin vassals declared him rightful heir.
Philip supported Arthur's claim to Plantagenet lands in France,
arraigned John for marrying Isabella of Angoulême,
already promised to a certain Count of la Marche,
and prosecuted hostilities vigorously, his hand
being formidably strengthened by the mysterious disappearance of Arthur after capture by
his uncle. The great Château Gaillard fell
(1204) and, in a short time, Philip was master
of Brittany, Normandy, Maine, Anjou,
Touraine and Northern Poitou – while John
had no significant French territory outside
Guyenne and Southern Poitou. Philip's final
triumph came in 1214 with the defeat of the
English and Imperial forces at Bouvines, decisive for the history of the French Nation.

Meanwhile, despite the interdict laid on
France by Innocent III (1200) because of the

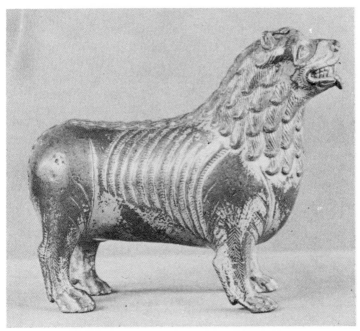

Aquamanile in the form of a Lion. French School *c.* 1200
*(National Gallery of Art, Washington D.C. Widener Collection)*

King's irregular marriage with Agnes of Meran, other events occurred from which Philip profited. Warlike Frenchmen absented themselves in 1202, on the discreditable Fourth Crusade, and sacked Constantinople. The heretics of Southern France, whose way of life combined spiritual qualities with social dangers, turned deaf ears to the preaching of Cistercian monks and the exhortations of Saint Dominic, bringing upon themselves the cruel slaughter of the Albigensian War (1209–1229), in which Simon de Montfort, father of "the founder of the English House of Commons", made conquests which the French crown would subsequently exploit.

At the time of his death, in 1223, Philip Augustus might have said, as Saint Louis would say later, "there is only one King in France". His legacy to the country will be considered under the next reign.

Louis VIII
*(Bibliothèque Nationale, Estampes, Paris)*

# LOUIS VIII, 1223–1226

## (Son of PHILIP II and Isabella of Hainault)

Born 1187, was 35 when he ascended the throne, and 39 when he died.

Married Blanche of Castile by whom he had numerous children, including:

> LOUIS IX (Saint Louis)
>
> Robert, Count of Artois
>
> Alphonse, Count of Poitou and Toulouse – married Joan, daughter of Raymond VII of Toulouse
>
> Charles, Count of Anjou, Maine, Provence and Forcalquier; King of Sicily, titular King of Jerusalem – married (1) Beatrice of Provence, (2) Margaret of Burgundy

*Thumbnail Sketch* A small bundle of nervous energy, whose sobriquet – "the Lion" – was applicable to the spirit rather than the body.

## WHAT TO KNOW

Philip Augustus had demonstrated his confidence in the future and solidity of the Capet dynasty by breaking with the family custom which had hitherto ensured that the heir was crowned in his predecessor's lifetime. Louis VIII underwent this ceremony at Rheims on 6 August 1223, some three weeks after his father's death, and, retaining the counsellors of the previous reign, devoted himself to a continuation of parental policy: expulsion of the English and territorial expansion.

A brisk descent was soon made upon Southern Poitou; its main harbour – La Rochelle (for the English an important point of entry into France) – was captured in 1224; the whole province then fell into the French King's hands, which meant that Plantagenet continental power was now restricted to Guyenne.

The fair land of Languedoc beckoned next. Here, as in Provence, heresy was by no means dead. The optimism with which the human dilemma was inevitably regarded in this sun-drenched country-side, where freedom, poetry and wealth made for joy rather than fear, where the conception of an after-life impinged lightly upon the present, and where connections with the Levant and Moorish Spain stimulated dangerous thoughts, continued to present the medieval Church with a difficult row to hoe. When Pope Honorius III invited Louis to smite these enemies of the Lord, and Amaury de Montfort confessed himself incapable of holding down the territory conquered by his father, the opportunity for a permanent extension of royal power in this area seemed too good to miss. Louis moved south down the Rhône, subjected Avignon to a three months' siege and paid dearly for his success with disastrous casualties from the variety of diseases generally designated as "camp fever". When autumn brought the campaigning season to a close the King withdrew, only to succumb to the prevalent dysentery, of which he died at Montpensier in the Auvergne on 8 November 1226. But the expedition had benefited the French monarchy – three years later Languedoc was to be firmly under the Capet crown.

Louis VIII, despite his obvious services to the dynasty, left it in a state which might well have precipitated crisis. A seemingly inconsistent and unwise will, executed some seventeen months before his death, divided his territories dangerously amongst his sons – as demonstrated by their titles recorded on the previous page. He drew his last breath in a state of deep concern about the succession, reiterating a death-bed instruction that Louis, his eleven-year-old heir, should be sustained by the immediate rendering of homage and by the safeguard of an early coronation.

The thirteenth century saw France enjoy a high flowering of culture. Trades and crafts, fostered by the guilds and the great fairs, flourished, the tentacles of commerce stretched far, pilgrims enjoyed the road to Rome and the "Milky Way" to

(Photo des Musées Nationaux)
The Confinement (Chartres Cathedral)

Compostella. The essentially out-going orders of Friars Minor
(founded by Saint Francis in 1209) and Friars Preachers (founded
by Saint Dominic in 1216) played an important role in the intellectual renaissance of the time, and accorded better with contemporary taste than the more inward-looking monasteries, which had
also made an incalculable contribution to French and European
civilization. The University of the growing city of Paris attracted
scholars of distinction: the Dominican Saint Thomas Aquinas,
the Franciscans Saint Bonaventure and Roger Bacon amongst
others. French began to be a literary language, whilst the
triumphant Gothic architecture of Beauvais, Amiens, Rheims,
Paris, Chartres, Bourges and Saint Louis' jewel the Sainte-
Chapelle – exemplifies the artistic and technical genius of an
essentially God-centred age.

# RADIATING OR
# GEOMETRICAL GOTHIC
## (Gothique Rayonnant)
## 1226–1380

| | |
|---|---|
| Louis IX (Saint Louis) | 1226–1270 |
| Philip III (The Bold) | 1270–1285 |
| Philip IV (The Fair) | 1285–1314 |
| Louis X (The Quarrelsome) | 1314–1316 |
| John I | 1316 |
| Philip V (The Tall) | 1316–1322 |
| Charles IV (The Fair) | 1322–1328 |
| Philip VI | 1328–1350 |
| John II (The Good) | 1350–1364 |
| Charles V (The Wise) | 1364–1380 |

*(In England cf. DECORATED 1307–1377)*

| | |
|---|---|
| Henry III | 1216–1272 |
| Edward I | 1272–1307 |
| Edward II | 1307–1327 |
| Edward III | 1327–1377 |
| Richard II | 1377–1399 |

RADIATING OR GEOMETRICAL GOTHIC
Interior of Amiens Cathedral

# RADIATING or GEOMETRICAL GOTHIC (Gothique Rayonnant) 1226–1380

We now plunge into the age of faith, associated with the great revivals largely attributable to Saint Dominic (1170–1221) and Saint Francis of Assisi (1182–1226). In this period (and particularly during the thirteenth century) Gothic art attains its climax. Cathedrals rise to great heights – towering above the clustered dwellings of citizens – the eye is continually carried up, enlarged windows show circle after circle crowning and amalgamating with the lancets (thus creating the effect from which is derived the epithet "geometrical") and glow with sumptuous glass. You will tend to see more sculpture outside and more glass inside French than English cathedrals, largely due to the much greater wealth of the French monasteries and chapters, though it is also worth remembering that, despite her upheavals, France was spared Puritanism, and never suffered such prolonged and methodical iconoclasm as that perpetrated by Roundhead William Dowsing and his like.

You will now recall the old tag:

"Clocher de Chartres, nef d'Amiens,
Choeur de Beauvais, portail de Reims"

(Chartres' tower, Amiens' nave, Beauvais' choir, Rheims' portal), and remember that, while these great shrines were under construction, Saint Louis was crusading, the Teutonic Knights were carrying the cross East into heathen Prussia, Saint Thomas Aquinas was beating out the official doctrine of the Roman Catholic Church, and Dante was engaged upon *The Divine Comedy*.

Louis IX

*( Musée de Cluny, from the Sainte Chapelle, Paris. Mansell-Alinari )*

ING OR GEOMETRICAL GOTHIC 55

I
### (Son of LOUIS VIII and Blanche of Castile)

Born 1215, was 11 when he ascended the throne, and 55 when he
died.

Married Margaret of Provence by whom he had eleven children,
including:
> Isabella – married Theobald of Champagne, King of
> Navarre
> PHILIP III (The Bold)
> Robert, Count of Clermont, Lord of Bourbon – married
> Beatrice of Burgundy, Lady of Bourbon – *from them
> sprang the House of Bourbon.*

*Thumbnail Sketch*   Saint Louis combined pious asceticism with a
gay and genial charm. Though capable of formidable anger his
humanity and passion for justice were real. An absolutist by pro-
found intellectual and religious conviction, this monarch is the
personification of medievalism at its noblest.

## WHAT TO KNOW

Louis IX succeeded in a moment of crisis. He was a minor, the
Regent (his mother, Blanche of Castile) suffered from the apparent
disadvantages of femininity and foreign extraction, which she
swiftly overcame, but it is not surprising that disgruntled feudatories seized what they felt to be a chance to reassert independence.
Blanche, intelligent, determined and pious, submitted her son to
a rigorous education, to teach him to be a king, but also established
herself as the real ruler of France until her death in 1253.

Supported by the Church, by the city of Paris and other powerful
towns, Blanche rounded sharply on the menacing combination of
rebel lords: Raymond of Toulouse, Peter Mauclerc of Brittany
and Theobald of Champagne, led by Richard of Cornwall,
adventurous brother of Henry III of England. In Theobald she
excited a passion which won him to her, and delighted contemporary satirists (her daughter Isabella married his son and name-
sake); the others submitted. Tracts of Languedoc came to the
French crown and it was agreed that Louis' brother Alphonse

should marry Joan of Toulouse, Raymond's daughter and heiress, which brought further valuable acquisitions on the death of that nobleman in 1249. (Treaty of Meaux, 1229.) Peace was made with the remaining insurgents at Saint-Aubin-du-Cormier in 1231 and in 1234 Louis was married to Margaret of Provence, thus further strengthening the dynasty's grip upon the South. In 1236 the twenty-one-year-old King became associated with his mother as ruler, but policy remained unchanged and a baronial revolt, assisted by Henry III of England, was crushed by Louis at Taillebourg and Saintes (1242), important engagements in the long effort to break feudalism. 1244 saw the last of the Albigensians burned in the dramatic castle of Montségur, high above the valley of the Aude, and, in 1245, Provence fell to Louis' brother Charles (later to be King of Sicily and titular King of Jerusalem) through his marriage with Louis' sister-in-law Beatrice.

In 1248 Louis, grateful for recovery from illness and fulfilling an ambition doubtless long cherished, embarked at Aigues-Mortes, with pilgrim's staff and *Oriflamme*, for Egypt. The Seventh Crusade, notable for the seizure of Damietta and the untidy battle of Mansourah, ended in much slaughter of common soldiery and the capture of King and nobles. Louis, ransomed, then spent almost four years in Palestine strengthening garrisons, castles and ports, until his mother's death recalled him. He reached Hyères in July 1254.

The achievements of the last sixteen years of the reign constitute Louis' claim to fame. Above all he captured the imagination of contemporaries and posterity as the Great Justiciary. His prohibition of judicial combat led to a vast increase of appeals, first from the domain, but spreading ever further as the reputation of the King's courts grew, and leaving the picture of an infinitely accessible Solomon-figure under the oak at Vincennes. Similarly royal coinage began to replace the inferior specie minted by feudatories, while *enquêteurs* (recalling Charlemagne's *Missi*

Enamel plaque. Saints rising from their tombs. Mid-thirteenth century
*(Victoria and Albert Museum. Crown Copyright)*

*Dominici* and foreshadowing Richelieu's *intendants*) toured the
land to correct incompetence and malpractice. Nor was Louis'
judicial reputation restricted to France, though the *Mise of
Amiens* (1264) whereby he freed Henry III from the shackles of
the Provisions of Oxford, proved an abortive attempt to support
royal authority. In addition to this the period, though not univer-
sally prosperous, saw the fortification of Carcassonne, technical
triumphs by Gothic master-builders, the prose chronicles of
Villehardouin and Joinville, the allegorical poem *Le Roman de la
Rose*, the development of universities (Robert de Sorbon founded
in 1257 the College later known as the Sorbonne) and a remarkable spread of the French language in Europe. In foreign relations
Louis thought in terms of peace on the frontiers and death to the
Saracen. He made border adjustments with James I of Aragon and
ceded lands marching with Guyenne to Henry III, while the
latter renounced all other territorial claims in France.

But 1270 saw Louis once again captivated by the false glamour of
a crusade, and thus it was that the founder of French absolutism,
he whom Matthew Paris designated "the King of Kings", perished
under the August sun before Tunis, reaping the reward of
canonization twenty-seven years later.

Philip III
*(Bibliothèque Nationale, Estampes, Paris)*

## PHILIP III (THE BOLD), 1270–1285
### (Son of LOUIS IX and Margaret of Provence)

Born 1245, was 25 when he ascended the throne, and 40 when he died.

Married Isabella of Aragon by whom he had five children, including:

> PHILIP IV (The Fair)
> Charles, Count of Valois, Alençon, Chartres and Le Perche,
> *from whom sprang the House of Valois*

Married Mary of Brabant, by whom he had three children:

> Louis, Count of Evreux
> Margaret, married Edward I, King of England
> Blanche, married Rudolf of Hapsburg

*Thumbnail Sketch* A pious, courageous knight – but unintelligent, and, except in his devotion to Mary of Brabant, monkish.

### WHAT TO KNOW

The casualties of the ill-fated Tunisian crusade included not only Saint Louis but also Philip III's first queen – Isabella of Aragon – together with his uncle and aunt – Alphonse and Joan of Poitou and Toulouse. Since these two were childless the broad acres of Poitou, and most of Languedoc, now became part of the royal domain – with the exception of the Agenais, on the Garonne, which went to England's Edward I by the Treaty of Amiens (1273), and the Comtat-Venaissin, with its noble capital of Avignon, which remained in papal hands until 1790.

In 1274 there died a prince with the promising name of Henry of Navarre, younger son of the pot-bellied Theobald of Champagne whose relationship with Blanche of Castile had given rise to such hilarious scurrility. His infant daughter Joan was now brought to Philip's court, a court which was to witness great advances in culture after the marriage of its essentially simple monarch with Mary of Brabant – though the hanging of Philip's favourite, Peter de la Brosse, an ambitious parvenu whose elevation from the status of surgeon-barber to the rank of Chamberlain had aroused the enmity of Queen and nobles, makes an ugly story. This Joan was to marry, ten years later, Philip's eldest son and heir, who would become Philip IV. For the time being Navarre, despite the opposition of Castile, was administered by France, and the crowns of the two countries were to be united for a spell on the accession of Philip III's grandson, Louis X, in 1314.

In the later part of his reign Philip fell deeply under the influence of his uncle, Charles of Anjou, who had accepted the crown of Naples and Sicily, offered him by Pope Urban IV, in 1265. This brother of Saint Louis, whose wide-ranging ambitions included the capture of Constantinople and the domination of the Levant, raised up against himself a coalition which included Pope Nicholas III, the Eastern Emperor Michael Palaeologus, Peter III of Aragon and a number of Sicilian nobles. The death of Nicholas in 1280 and the election of Martin IV (Simon de Brie – a creature of Charles) offered a temporary respite, but, in 1282, French brutality and tyranny provoked in Palermo the rebellion known to historians, and admirers of the composer Verdi, as "The Sicilian Vespers". The rising spread, Peter of Aragon assisted the insurgents and wrested Sicily from the Angevins, who continued to rule in Naples, however, until 1442, when that kingdom, also, fell into Aragonese hands. Charles of Anjou, whose disastrously tempting claim to Naples would later be revived by Charles VIII and Louis XII, raged impotently, accomplished the improbable gastronomic feat of consuming his sceptre, and died at Foggia early in 1285.

Philip must needs avenge him by chastising Peter III. Out came the *Oriflamme* and into Aragon the French marched. Elne was captured and its inhabitants massacred with crusading zeal. Gerona was besieged and eventually taken. But the army had sustained severe losses, sickness was rife, the supporting fleet was destroyed by Roger de Loria – in grim weather the invaders withdrew. They enjoyed the doubtful distinction of constituting the

Polyptych. Virgin and Child enthroned. French 1250–1300. Silver gilt,
decorated with niello and ivory

*(The Metropolitan Museum of Art, New York. Gift of J. Pierpont Morgan, 1917.)*

first French force to wage aggressive war in Europe. But the
King, of whom the most that can be said is that he was a pale
reflection of Saint Louis, succumbed to fever at Perpignan on
5 October 1285.

## PHILIP IV (THE FAIR), 1285–1314
(Son of PHILIP III and Isabella of Aragon)

Born 1268, was 17 when he ascended the throne, and 46 when he died.

Married Joan of Champagne and Navarre by whom he had four children:

> LOUIS X (The Quarrelsome)
> Isabella – married Edward II, King of England
> PHILIP V (The Tall)
> CHARLES IV (The Fair)

*Thumbnail Sketch* Handsome, cold, intelligent and mysterious – this monarch found it possible to combine the rigours of conventional piety with ruthless and efficient power politics.

### WHAT TO KNOW

The inherited hostilities with Aragon were ended by the Treaty of Tarascon in 1292 – but the same year saw Norman and English sailors at each others' throats, which drove Philip IV to an attempted solution of the Plantagenet problem by the seizure of Gascony (1294) and the conclusion with Scotland's John Balliol of what would later be called "The Auld Alliance" against Edward I (1295). The proceedings, however, were perfunctory; a truce, mediated by Pope Boniface VIII, was achieved in 1297, to be converted into peace two years later at Montreuil-sur-Mer. Further negotiations culminated in 1303, leaving Edward his status as Duke of Aquitaine and the hand in marriage of Margaret, Philip's sister, while the boy who would be Edward II was betrothed to Philip's daughter, Isabella. From these nuptials arose the claims which precipitated the Hundred Years War.

Philip had been freed, by the truce, to turn on Guy, Count of Flanders, who had befriended Edward I. Early successes encouraged an attempt to exploit this rich province profitably and unscrupulously. However, the sturdy Flemings rose in 1302 and emulated "The Sicilian Vespers" by a wholesale slaughter of Frenchmen known as "The Bruges Mattins". In the same year they defeated their persecutors at Courtrai, but Philip was able to restore the military situation at Mons-en-Pévèle (1304), being lucky to emerge with Flanders still under his feudal wing, and the possession of Béthune, Lille, Orchies and Douai.

Unsatisfactory finance was the bugbear of the French monarchy and, indeed, a major cause of its eventual fall. Philip IV, as the result of war, of the territorial growth of the royal domain and of increasingly sophisticated administrative machinery, was always in desperate need of money. In addition to this his middle-class advisers, Peter Flote and, later, William of Nogaret, influenced him by their study of Roman Law, with its emphasis on centralized absolutism. The bull *Clericis Laicos* of 1296, whereby ecclesiastics were not to pay secular taxes without the consent of the Pope, by no means accorded with "the pleasure of the King" and brought him into conflict with that irascible old pontiff Boniface VIII, who also had caesarist ideas. The export of bullion was forbidden; the papal legate – Bernard de Saisset, Bishop of Pamiers – was arrested on a treason charge; the Holy Father, elated by the Jubilee demonstrations of the year 1300, summoned French bishops to Rome to discipline their King. Philip countered by calling, for what is generally regarded as the first time, the "Estates General" of France (see note page 72) as a demonstration of national solidarity (1302). Next year Philip was excom-

municated, an interdict was imminent – so William of Nogaret left secretly for Italy. There he made contact with Boniface's enemy Sciarra Colonna, arrested the Pope at Anagni, but was forced to yield up his prisoner in face of a popular rising. Shortly afterwards Boniface died, was succeeded by Benedict XI, who in his turn was followed by Bertrand de Goth, Archbishop of Bordeaux, who took the name of Clement V and whose memory is enshrined in the Graves vineyards at Château Pape Clément. He installed himself in the city of Avignon (a name of magic to those who have drunk Châteauneuf in the shadow of the papal palace), but also in the pocket of the French King, thus starting

Great Seal of Philip IV (*Mansell Collection*)

The Fleur de Lys, an attribute of French royalty since the twelfth century, has ornamented objects of Egyptian, Greek and Roman antiquity as well as being found in Germany, Spain and England. Its origin has been fancifully traced to a lily proffered at the baptism of Clovis (496) by a visiting angel, and to the representation of the Holy Spirit as a dove turned upside down! It is, in fact, probably derived from the sceptre heads of the Frankish Kings.

the "Babylonish Captivity", which lasted from 1309 to 1378.

Having mulcted Jews and Lombard bankers, and having debased the coinage, Philip's triumph over the Papacy now made him feel strong enough to attack the Knights Templars, the anachronistic and wealthy crusading order which maintained some 5,000 members in France. Accused of a wide variety of crime and vice, from sacrilege to sodomy, weakened by worthless confessions extracted under torture, all suffered arrest and many were done to death. In 1312 the Order was dissolved and most of its riches passed into the coffers of the King of France.

Two years remained, years embittered by the matrimonial misdemeanours of the three Royal daughters-in-law, before Philip died at Fontainebleau from the effects of a hunting accident in November 1314. He left an increased domain and a strengthened France.

Loys Hutin, premier fils du Roy Philippe le Bel:
Et son petit fils Iean.

Louis X
*(Bibliothèque Nationale, Estampes, Paris)*

# LOUIS X (THE QUARRELSOME), 1314–1316
(Son of PHILIP IV and Joan of Champagne and Navarre)

Born 1289, was 25 when he ascended the throne, and 27 when he died.

Married Margaret of Burgundy by whom he had one daughter:
      Joan, Queen of Navarre, at first in her own right, and then
       associated with her husband Philip, Count of Evreux
Married Clemence of Hungary by whom he had one son:
     JOHN I

*Thumbnail Sketch*   The little that emerges about the character of this handsome young man suggests a frivolous play-boy.

## WHAT TO KNOW
Louis X, finding satisfaction in his private pleasures, virtually abandoned the government of the kingdom to his uncle, Charles of Valois, younger brother of Philip the Fair. Overmighty subjects, sore at the restrictions which the monarchy had been building up, reacted sharply against the royal servants of the previous reign, and the new King was persuaded to hang Enguerrand of Marigny, his father's shrewd Norman financial adviser, on the sinister Montfaucon gallows. Recrudescence of feudal chaos, famine, a brief inglorious campaign in the Flanders mud – such is the story of the reign, upon which a mild ray of light is shed by an edict against serfdom (1315), issued for profit as much as through altruism, in that freedom had to be purchased. In the same year Margaret of Burgundy, Louis' disgraced first wife, died in prison, leaving him a daughter, Joan, who may or may not have been legitimate. The King now married Clemence of Hungary, but draughts of wine incautiously consumed in a cool cellar at Vincennes after a heating ball-game led to his premature death, leaving no male heir – but a widow great with child.

Mention has already been made of the "increasingly sophisticated administrative machinery" of the French monarchy, and an opportunity now presents itself of considering an important institution: the Parliament of Paris.

In the first years of the Capet monarchy the King, surrounded by a court of chosen feudal vassals, whose right and obligation it was to proffer advice, dealt with all subjects concerning the government of the land. Expansion of Royal power inevitably meant increase of business, from which the natural developments are delegation and specialization. This process was at work in matters of justice as early as the reign of Louis VII, and by that of Philip the Fair the Parliament of Paris, the chief law court of France, consisting of Royal advisers and a growing class of legal experts, was in existence. Over the years, and for a variety of reasons, a principle of hereditary membership was established, to be finalized in the reign of Henry IV (1604) when an office became family property on payment of an annual tax called the *"Paulette"*, thus creating a powerful "Nobility of the Robe", with an esprit de corps born of permanent session, which augmented the privileged Second Estate of France (see note on the Estates General, page 72). Yet "this court was not a court alone". The Parliament, operating from a building on the site of the present Palais de Justice, concerned itself at one time or another, but always under the Royal aegis, with food, public health, education, commerce, industry, traffic, religious orthodoxy, censorship and the police – in fact with the whole domestic economy of the capital. It did not initiate legislation, in the sense that legislation came to be

initiated by the English Parliament at Westminster – but for the purposes of publicity and record it was found convenient that it should register on its files the edicts of the King. These edicts did not always meet with the approval of the critical lawyers, who would suggest amendments, and, on occasion, refuse registration by what were called "remonstrances". But the monarch could always get his way, in the end, by a ceremonial appearance in person in the *Grand' Chambre* of the Parliament, where he enforced his will by the procedure known as a *"Lit de Justice"* (Bed of Justice). With intervals of hostility, throne and Parliament co-operated during the greater part of the institution's long history

St. Michael. Carved wood. First half of fourteenth century
*(Victoria and Albert Museum. Crown Copyright)*

which came to an end with its suppression by the National
Assembly in 1790.

Philip V
*(Bibliothèque Nationale, Estampes, Paris)*

# JOHN I, 1316
### (Son of LOUIS X and Clemence of Hungary)

Born 15 November, died 23 November 1316.

# PHILIP V (THE TALL), 1316–1322
### (Son of PHILIP IV and Joan of Champagne and Navarre, brother of LOUIS X)

Born 1292, was 24 when he ascended the throne, and 30 when he died.

Married Joan of Burgundy by whom he had five children, including one son who died in infancy.

*Thumbnail Sketch*   From this short reign emerges the picture of a monarch swift in action, intelligent in administration and ruthless in persecution.

## WHAT TO KNOW

For the first time a Capet of the direct line had died without a male heir. It is true that Louis X had had a four-year-old daughter, Joan, but her tender age, and her mother's reputation, defeated her chances of succession. In this moment of crisis Philip, Count of Poitiers, brother to the late monarch, stole a march on his uncle, Charles of Valois, and was proclaimed Regent. All eyes turned upon the childbed of Clemence of Hungary. On 15 November 1316 she bore a son, John I, who died eight days later. Ambition and rough common sense suggested that Philip of Poitiers should now become King. His coronation at Rheims on 9 January 1317 was a comparatively ill-patronized function, attended by formidable security precautions. In the following month the accomplished fact was approved by the Estates, summoned to Paris, and justified by an appeal to the law of the Salian Franks (normally referred to as the Salic Law) whereby it was held that a woman might not inherit land. Joan's rights were disposed of by cash down and a pension.

The few years which remained to Philip produced peace with Flanders, some sensible regulations ensuring disciplined procedure by the judges of the Parliament of Paris, ordinances permitting the organization of citizens for the defence of towns – all calculated to win popular support for the monarchy against the great feudatories. But there was, too, widespread rural malaise, much persecution of Jews and wholesale slaughter of lepers – who were suspected of plotting to spread their fell disease – creating a background of gloom, against which Philip died on 3 January 1322.

### Note on the Estates General

The Estates General, a body of representatives of the three orders or classes into which France (like some other countries) divided itself, is generally regarded as having been first summoned by Philip IV in 1302 (see page 64).

The three orders, classes or "Estates" were,

(1) The Clergy.
(2) The Nobility.
(3) The Commons, who became known as the "Third Estate" (Tiers État).

The representatives were brought together as often, or as seldom, as the King wished, to a place of his choosing. Once assembled they attended Mass together, heard the monarch's opening and closing speeches together, but they deliberated entirely separately. In these sessions they considered, and expressed opinion upon, such

matters as had been brought up by their ruler. Further, they had the right to present lists of grievances, embodied in what were called *cahiers* or "quires", for the Royal attention – but the King was under no obligation to take action on their opinions or their complaints. Separate discussion, and the custom of voting by orders, put the Third Estate in a position of weakness, for its members would normally find themselves in a minority of 1 to 2 *vis-à-vis* the Clergy and the Nobility, who were natural allies bound together by the iniquitous privilege of virtual immunity from taxation. It is, thus, obvious that the Estates General did not achieve anything approaching the true representation of the people

Virgin and Child: group in painted limestone. About 1300–1330 –
from the Church at Saint Chéron, in eastern Champagne
*( The Metropolitan Museum of Art, New York. Fletcher Fund, 1939.)*

of France, nor was it so constituted as to be able to exercise
much influence over their destiny. Meetings became increasingly
infrequent as the Royal power developed – witness the fact that,
after the dismissal of the Estates in 1615, they were not called
again until 1789. "In France the Estates General were so managed
as to place the whole realm under royal absolutism." (Stubbs.)

Charles IV
*(Bibliothèque Nationale, Estampes, Paris)*

## CHARLES IV (THE FAIR), 1322–1328

(Son of PHILIP IV and Joan of Champagne and Navarre,
brother of LOUIS X and PHILIP V)

Born 1295, was 27 when he ascended the throne, and 33 when he
died.

Married Blanche of Burgundy (repudiated) by whom he had a
son and a daughter who died in infancy.
Married Mary of Luxembourg by whom he had a son who died
in infancy.
Married Joan of Evreux, by whom he had three children, including:

> Blanche – married Philip, Duke of Orleans, Count of
> Valois and Beaumont

*Thumbnail Sketch*   Except for the remarkable severity with which
he treated rebellious feudatories and untrustworthy public servants, this monarch leaves a dim impression.

### WHAT TO KNOW

Philip V had no male heir; once again recourse was had to the
Salic Law and the crown passed to a third brother – Charles,
Count of La Marche. It was rapidly clear that Charles IV would
give short shrift to disorderly feudatories, and the notorious lord
of Casaubon – de l'Ile Jourdain – soon swung from the Montfaucon gibbet. Next year, in 1324, the King once more took up
the struggle with England, and by 1326 had overrun most of
Aquitaine. However, the desire of Charles' sister Isabella to cross
the Channel, in order to intrigue with her lover Mortimer against
her unsatisfactory husband Edward II, opened the way to
negotiation. It was thereby agreed that France should keep the
Agenais (between the Dordogne and the Garonne) and that Prince
Edward (later Edward III) should do homage for the duchy. But
the hand of death (men whispered darkly of the curse of the dying
Templars) continued to fall rapidly upon the sons of Philip the
Fair. In 1328 Charles, sensing his fate, was inviting his first cousin
Philip of Valois to be guardian to his Queen and to her child, as
yet unborn – for Charles, too, had no son to follow him when he

died in that year. Subsequently Queen Joan gave birth to a daughter, which left the Barons and the "notables of Paris and the good towns" with another crisis on their hands. They were, of course, clear that the ruler must be a man. Edward III of England claimed the inheritance through his mother Isabella, daughter of Philip the Fair – but the assembled dignitaries greatly preferred a relation of the male line, in fact the guardian appointed by the late King, and the crown went to Philip of Valois. The stirrings of nationalism had pushed their choice towards a Frenchman rather than a foreigner. The Hundred Years War loomed ahead.

Thus ended the Capets of the direct line. Let the words of a French historian stand as their epitaph: "Between 987 and 1328 fourteen successive kings, all of the same family and descended in the direct line from the same ancestor, Hugh the Great, Duke of Francia, sat on the throne of France. During this epoch France was born . . . The Capetians . . . had united France, territorially, endowed monarchy with new vigour and renown, invested the crown with the halo of sanctity, created an administration which was to bind the kingdom together for centuries, and begun to accustom their subjects to feel alike and express themselves alike. The House of Capet had drafted the broad outlines of the French nation. It was for the future to complete the work." (Robert Fawtier, *The Capetian Kings of France*. Translated by Lionel Butler and R. J. Adam.)

Funeral mask of a woman

*( Musée d'Arras. Photo des Musées Nationaux)*

Philip VI, by Moncornet
*(Bibliothèque Nationale, Estampes, Paris)*

# PHILIP VI, 1328–1350

(Son of Charles of Valois, Alençon, Chartres and Le Perche –
titular Emperor of Constantinople – and Margaret of Sicily.
Nephew of PHILIP IV, cousin of CHARLES IV.)

Born 1293, was 35 when he ascended the throne, and 57 when he
died.

Married Joan of Burgundy by whom he had eight children, including:
> JOHN II· (The Good)
> Philip, Duke of Orleans and Touraine – married Blanche,
> daughter of CHARLES IV (The Fair)

Married Blanche of Navarre, by whom he had one daughter who
died young.

*Thumbnail Sketch*  A man of cultivated taste, impulsive courage
and formidable temper, who did France disservice by his amateur
attitude to the grim business of war.

## WHAT TO KNOW

The Valois line was, of course, directly descended from Hugh
Capet, and this house was now to rule France for two hundred and
sixty-one years, until another succession of three sonless brothers
would necessitate a cast-back, this time to the Bourbon collateral,
in whose veins the same blood ran.

The reign opened auspiciously enough. Philip assisted the feck-
less Louis, Count of Flanders, by defeating the latter's rebellious
subjects at Cassel in 1328, and had the pleasure, next year, of
receiving young Edward III's homage for his French possessions
at Amiens. But peace with England was not to be preserved. David
II of Scotland, son of Robert Bruce, had been sent as a refugee to
the French court, where he found traditional support against the
Sassenach. The disaffected Robert of Artois, banished from France,
crossed the Channel and poured anti-Philip propaganda into
Edward's ear. In 1336 the French King persuaded Louis of
Flanders to arrest English merchants in his territories. Edward III
promptly replied by stopping the wool exports upon which the
cloth weavers of Bruges, Ypres and Ghent depended. The business-

like Flemish burghers, under their brewer leader Jacob van Artevelde, turned to England, where causes like the Gascon wine trade, the attraction of plunder and the more deep-rooted necessity for expansion, made hostilities welcome, and persuaded Edward to claim the French crown through his mother Isabella, daughter of Philip the Fair. The Hundred Years War, waged sporadically from 1337 to 1453, began.

The English already took a highly professional view of the military art, whereas to the French it was still a chivalrous, religious, upper-class, sporting exercise. To both sides it came naturally – for rivalry had been continuous since William of Normandy had landed at Pevensey in 1066. In 1340 Edward cleared the seas by defeating Philip's Italian-manned fleet at Sluys. Next year a disputed succession to the Duchy of Brittany enabled Philip to support Joan of Penthièvre while Edward backed Joan of Montfort, as these determined ladies did battle on behalf of their imprisoned husbands. Truce, treachery and murder followed until in 1346 the English, persuaded by the disgruntled French Lord of Harcourt, were on the Continent once more, with a force in which infantry predominated. Tactical skill, discipline, the hiss of cloth-yard shafts and the bang of small field-pieces, discharged by men of low degree, tumbled the picturesque French knights at Crécy, thus writing a page of social as much as of military history. A subject for Rodin was then provided by Eustache de St. Pierre, Jean d'Aire, Jacques and Pierre de Vissant, and two other gallant burghers of Calais, which, after wholesale eviction of its population and an influx of Edward's subjects, became an English town and an invaluable bridgehead from 1347 until 1558.

In the years 1348–1349 the horrors of war were succeeded by the ravages of the Black Death, naïvely attributed to the poisoning of wells by the Jews, who were consequently slaughtered in great numbers. Flagellants roamed the devastated countryside hoping to turn away the wrath of God by excoriating their backs with scourges and their interiors with a diet

Scene of courtly life – about 1360. The Betrothal Kiss. French School of
Provence. Fourteenth century
*(Louvre, Paris. Photo des Musées Nationaux)*

of nails and fire. Under-populated and over-taxed – France
groaned. Territorially speaking two feeble rays of light enliven the
gloom. Dauphiné was purchased in 1349 – the area of south-
eastern France immediately North of Provence, so-called from the
use of the name *Dauphin* (Dolphin) in its ruling family for some two
hundred years. This title now attached itself to the eldest sons of
the Kings of France, whose perquisite the province became. The
year 1350 saw another sale – that of the important town of Mont-
pellier, by the house of Aragon.

In the midst of this considerable misery Philip VI died, at
Nogent-le-Roi, North of Chartres, on 22 August 1350.

John II
*(Louvre, Paris. Photo Giraudon)*

# JOHN II (THE GOOD), 1350–1364
(Son of PHILIP VI and Joan of Burgundy)

Born 1319, was 31 when he ascended the throne, and 44 when he died.

Married Bonne of Luxembourg, by whom he had eleven children, including:

> CHARLES V
>
> Louis, Duke of Anjou, titular King of Naples, Sicily and Jerusalem
>
> John, Duke of Berry (of *The Very Rich Hours*)
>
> Philip the Bold, Duke of Burgundy
>
> Joan – married Charles the Bad, King of Navarre
>
> Isabella – married John Galeazzo Visconti, Duke of Milan

Married Joan of Auvergne whose children by him died in infancy.

*Thumbnail Sketch*   A monarch who combined the romantic and generous virtues with the foolish and ignorant vices of contemporary chivalry. He lacked mental, moral and political balance and was "Good" only in the sense of good fellowship.

## WHAT TO KNOW

John II opened his reign violently by executing as a traitor Raoul of Brienne, Constable of France, and recently a prisoner of the English, whom he replaced by a favourite cousin, Charles of La Cerda. To the latter he gave Angoulême, thus infuriating another kinsman, Charles of Navarre, who laid claim to that duchy. This second Charles – an agreeable and intelligent person of unscrupulous character – had earned his title "the Bad" for his brutality to the Navarrese rebels who rose in 1350. As great grandson to Philip the Bold, through Louis, Count of Evreux, and as grandson to Louis X, through that monarch's only daughter, he also cast eyes on the French crown, and, unappeased by marriage with Joan, John the Good's eight-year-old child, he murdered La Cerda in 1354. Two years later he was arrested whilst carousing with the Dauphin at Rouen, and, though incarcerated first in the Château Gaillard and subsequently in the Châtelet, was rapidly in touch with Edward III of England through his brother Philip and the Harcourt family.

The war had, in fact, been dragging on. The Order of the Garter had been founded by Edward in 1348, that of the Star by John in 1352, and French and English knights had hacked each other to death in futile chivalrous fashion at the famous "Battle of the Thirty" in Brittany in 1351. It was time for a return to professionalism and, in 1356, the Black Prince advanced northward from Guyenne with the grand strategic concept of bringing the greater part of Western France under English control. Unable to force a crossing of the Loire he withdrew some sixty miles, followed by King John, and inflicted upon him, at Poitiers, the most severe defeat yet suffered by the French at English hands. Casualties were heavy, the monarch disappeared into sumptuous captivity, and Froissart recorded the contemptuous hatred with which the militarily incompetent nobility were now regarded.

In this crisis the eighteen-year-old Dauphin (later Charles V) called the Estates General to Paris where a great popular municipal leader, Etienne Marcel, was organizing the citizens of the capital for defence. The Estates, led by Marcel and Robert Le Coq, Bishop of Laon, advocated measures of a democratic nature which, could they have found general support in the sorely divided country, would have altered the history of France. But it was not to be. Anti-Valois feeling led to the release of the charming but untrustworthy Charles the Bad, the struggle swung to and fro between him and the Dauphin and developed into civil war. Unhappy peasants, mercilessly dunned for money to ransom their worthless lords, rose in an insurrection called the *Jacquerie*, which was sternly put down, and Marcel was murdered (1358) when about to hand Paris over to Navarre. Once again Edward III crossed the Channel, but the Dauphin avoided military contact. By 1360 all were weary, the two Charleses came to terms, and the Treaty of Brétigny was agreed with Edward III. He gave up his claim to the French crown but, once again, secured the great mass of Aquitaine, stretching from near the Loire to the Pyrenees and, up in Picardy, retained his Calais bridgehead, the neighbouring

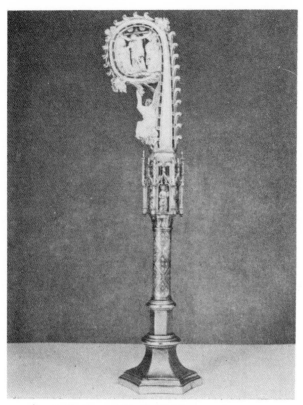

Head of a Pastoral Staff. Mid-fourteenth century
*(Victoria and Albert Museum. Crown Copyright)*

town of Guines and, some fifty miles to the South, the district of
Ponthieu. King John's ransom was fixed at 3,000,000 golden
crowns, to which Galeazzo Visconti, of Milan, subscribed
generously in return for the hand of the Princess Isabella in mar-
raige with his son John – yet another ground for subsequent French
interference in Italy. Pursuing mistaken policies to the end the
King now laid up further trouble by giving Burgundy to his son
Philip the Bold and, learning that his second son, the Duke of
Anjou, left in England as a hostage, had escaped, returned
quixotically to his golden cage in 1364 and died on 8 April during
the hospitable knightly junketings which greeted his arrival.

Charles V
*(Bibliothèque Nationale, Estampes, Paris)*

# CHARLES V (THE WISE), 1364–1380

(Son of JOHN II and Bonne of Luxembourg)

Born 1337, was 27 when he ascended the throne, and 43 when he died.

Married Joan of Bourbon, by whom he had eight children, including:

CHARLES VI

Louis, Duke of Touraine, Orléans and Valois – married Valentina Visconti, daughter of John Galeazzo Visconti and Isabella of France (see page 83).

*Thumbnail Sketch* Weak in body but powerful in mind, a great patron of the arts, this ruler exercised a despotism tempered by enlightenment.

## WHAT TO KNOW

The not inexperienced Charles V faced a number of problems which could only be solved by hostilities. Though personally unsuited to feats of arms this scholarly planner appreciated, as well as any soldier, the military importance of fortifications, artillery, pay, discipline and morale. He could also find able subordinates – and selected Bertrand Du Guesclin, a Breton squire, who saw through the humbug of chivalry with an instinctive understanding of the realities of war, to lead his new-look, non-feudal army. This tough professional imposed peace upon Charles of Navarre and was then directed to intervene against the Mont-fort faction and their English allies in the succession struggle which had ravaged Brittany since 1341. But Charles of Blois, the French choice, charged to his death with a rashness which also caused Du Guesclin's capture (Auray 1364) and France must needs accept the Treaty of Guérande whereby John of Montfort received the Duchy as Charles V's vassal. Du Guesclin was ransomed and set to work again.

Contemporary France suffered from the systematic plunder and brutal pleasures of the "Great Companies", composed of soldiers from many lands, unemployed since the Treaty of Brétigny. Charles sought to extirpate these pests and to attack the monstrous

Pedro the Cruel of Castile, ally of Edward the Black Prince, Duke of Aquitaine, and future father-in-law of John of Gaunt. So Du Guesclin led the companies beyond the Pyrenees, the fortunes of war swung to and fro, once again the formidable Breton suffered capture and required ransom, but, by 1369, Pedro lay dead and his bastard half-brother, the pro-French Henry of Trastamara, wore the Castilian crown.

It was now the turn of the English. The Duke of Aquitaine (the Black Prince) levied a hearth tax against which his vassals appealed to the overlord Charles V. Charles called the Prince to Paris, who offered to come "bassinet on head and with 60,000 men", which meant war. Charles ordered a prosaic strategy of scorched earth, maintenance of strongholds and refusal of battle. The French sat tight in fortified towns while the English, unable to find and destroy the enemy army, marched and counter-marched blazing a profitless trail of gutted farms and smoking villages. The Black Prince, militarily frustrated and wracked with malaria, subjected Limoges to sack and massacre (1370), Henry of Trastamara inflicted severe defeat on an English fleet off La Rochelle (1372), and by 1375 England's sole Continental possessions were Calais, Cherbourg, Brest, Bordeaux and Bayonne – and a two-year truce was declared. In 1377 Charles, a believer in naval as in military

power, demonstrated his strength by raids on the English coast. At home he tried, and failed, to acquire Brittany and, when he died, was combating rebellion in Languedoc and Flanders.

Over the latter province Charles had made a rare, and venial, political error. In 1369 he welcomed the marriage of his brother Philip of Burgundy (see page 83) with Margaret, heiress to the Count of Flanders, who brought with her Flanders, Artois, Rethel, Nevers and Franche Comté. Charles no doubt hoped to swing these lands into the French orbit; instead the ambitious Dukes created a Brussels–Dijon axis, which was to prove a menace to France subsequently.

Eight years later, in the South, Gregory XI,

Cup of Charles V
*(By permission of the Trustees of the British Museum)*

seventh Pope to reside at Avignon, moved, encouraged by Saint Catherine of Siena, to Rome, thus replacing the "Babylonish Captivity" (1309–1378) by the "Great Schism" (1378–1415), when rival pontiffs split the loyalties of Europe and abused one another across the 450 miles which separate the Patrimony of St. Peter from Provence.

Domestically the reign had been of great importance. The King patronized literature, employed translators and left material which would later enrich the Bibliothèque Nationale, while his architectural interests are exemplified by the chapel of Vincennes and the most famous of all Bastilles. Reformed coinage and reduced administrative expenditure brought economic recovery, and a reasonably fixed revenue for the Crown, though the imposition of internal customs dues and the continued sale of offices suggest that Charles V was not a financial genius. Above all, during these momentous years, feudalism had retreated further before the advance of the modernizing absolute monarchy.

# FLAMBOYANT GOTHIC
## (Style Flamboyant)
### 1380–1515

| | |
|---|---|
| Charles VI | 1380–1422 |
| Charles VII | 1422–1461 |
| Louis XI | 1461–1483 |
| Charles VIII | 1483–1498 |
| Louis XII | 1498–1515 |

*(In England cf. PERPENDICULAR 1377–1485)*

| | |
|---|---|
| Richard II | 1377–1399 |
| Henry IV | 1399–1413 |
| Henry V | 1413–1422 |
| Henry VI | 1422–1461 |
| Edward IV | 1461–1470 |
| Henry VI (restored) | 1470–1471 |
| Edward IV | 1471–1483 |
| Edward V | 1483 |
| Richard III | 1483–1485 |
| Henry VII | 1485–1509 |
| Henry VIII | 1509–1547 |

**FLAMBOYANT GOTHIC**
West front of the church of Saint Maclou, Rouen

*(Archives Photographiques, Paris)*

# FLAMBOYANT GOTHIC
## (Style Flamboyant)
### 1380–1515

Once again we have the inevitable date overlap, for, despite Renaissance influences, we find examples of the Flamboyant Gothic style well into the seventeenth century. But this is not to be wondered at. Thomas à Kempis (1380–1471) was an essentially medieval man, while Niccolo Machiavelli (1469–1527) could hardly have been more modern. Yet they were alive at the same time, and our period embraces both *The Imitation of Christ* (1418) and *The Prince* (1513).

But, as far as French architecture is concerned, it is as if men had said, once Beauvais was completed (1347), "We've gone about as high as we can go – how shall we now demonstrate our energy and ingenuity?" In the Flamboyant style they found the answer. Look at Saint-Maclou (Rouen), look at Saint-Germain-l'Auxerrois (Paris) – remembering its connection with the massacre of Saint Bartholomew – and you will see. Above all you will note frequent use of the ogee arch – the French call it *"l'arc en accolade"* (see page 37). It has doubly curved sides, the lower part of each side being concave and the upper part convex. And, as you look at the windows, you will see traceries rising like tongues of flame (hence the title of the style) and find a greater elaboration of decoration than at any stage yet.

Though it is, perhaps, natural in a consideration of France in the Middle Ages to give pride of place to her great churches, secular building should not be overlooked. Many small castles were destroyed by Richelieu – but medieval military architecture can still be studied at the Château Gaillard, Vincennes, Chinon and Carcassonne while, at Bourges, the famous house of Jacques Coeur bears witness to a high degree of domestic civilization.

Charles VI, by L. Gautier
*(Bibliothèque Nationale, Estampes, Paris)*

## CHARLES VI, 1380–1422

### (Son of CHARLES V and Joan of Bourbon)

Born 1368, was 11 when he ascended the throne, and 53 when he died.

Married Isabella of Bavaria, by whom he had ten children, including:

> Isabella – married Richard II of England and subsequently Charles, Duke of Orleans
>
> Joan – married John, Duke of Brittany and Count of Montfort
>
> Michelle – married Philip the Good, Duke of Burgundy
>
> Catherine – married Henry V of England and subsequently Sir Owen Tudor. Grandmother of Henry VII of England
>
> CHARLES VII

*Thumbnail Sketch*   A not unattractive boy – but lacking serious-ness, robustness and stability. From 1392 onwards much more frequently mad than sane.

### WHAT TO KNOW

The enchanting pages of the *Very Rich Hours of the Duke of Berry* (1416) gleam with opulent elegance, and we do well to remember that this reign, clouded by royal insanity, civil strife and national defeat, also saw handsome building, exquisite sculpture, distin-guished scholarship and the last twenty-four years of the life of Froissart!

The accession of the boy Charles VI was appreciated as an opportunity for profit by his uncles – the Dukes of Anjou, Berry, Burgundy and Bourbon – whose unscrupulous exactions soon led to revolts of the *Jacquerie* type. An insurrection in Ghent, raised by Philip Van Artevelde, brought Philip the Bold of Bur-gundy to the aid of his father-in-law, the Count of Flanders, followed enthusiastically by the young King. The French killed Van Artevelde and defeated his burghers at Roosebek (1382), so monarch and dukes could return jubilantly to chastise the dis-affected Parisians, whose own civic ambitions had been stirred by the pretensions of the Flemings.

In 1385 Charles married the attractive Isabella of Bavaria. Her insatiable appetite for an extensive repertoire of pleasures may have affected his stability but, momentarily, the situation improved. After an abortive plan to invade England and an ineffective declaration of war, the uncles were dismissed and the King ruled with his father's advisers. In 1392 an attempt was made on the life of one of these, Oliver Clisson, Constable of France. Peter Craon, the criminal, sought asylum with the Duke of Brittany, upon whom Charles now marched. On his way, however, he was so unnerved by a wild peasant prophesying treachery that he instantly killed four of his companions and only regained sanity for short intervals during the remainder of his life.

Once again it was the day of the Dukes. Their struggles eventually resolved themselves into deadly rivalry between John the Fearless of Burgundy, who succeeded his father Philip the Bold in 1404, and Louis of Orleans, the King's younger brother. The causes of discord were many. Burgundy saw England's friendship as commercially desirable for his Flemish subjects, Orleans longed to fight the ancient enemy; Burgundy, with an eye to Parisian opinion, took no side over the Great Schism, Orleans supported the Avignon Pope Benedict XIII. Both of them passionately coveted supreme power in France. In 1407 Orleans was murdered and Burgundy brazenly accepted responsibility for this act.

And now there is a change of nomenclature. Louis of Orleans' successor had been married into the Armagnac family, and it was as between Burgundians and Armagnacs that the struggle continued. The Burgundians found support, outside their own territories, in Paris and the North; Armagnac power, which controlled King and Dauphin, was rooted in the rest of France, particularly south of the Loire.

France, rent asunder, offered a tempting target to England's Henry V who, after a successful descent upon Harfleur (near Le

The Trinity. Morse (Cope clasp).
Franco-Burgundian, *c.* 1400
*(National Gallery of Art, Washington D.C. Widener Collection)*

Havre), decided to march his dysentery-ridden army to meet his
fleet at Calais. An Armagnac feudal host, forgetful of Du
Guesclin's lessons, lay across his road near Agincourt where, on
25 October 1415, it suffered disastrous defeat. Charles of Orleans,
the King's nephew, fell into English hands, but the factions
continued their massacre and counter-massacre, while Henry
campaigned systematically in Normandy. An attempted Bur-
gundian-Armagnac reconciliation was shattered by the murder
of John the Fearless, at a meeting with the Dauphin on the
bridge at Montereau, in 1419, which put his son and successor,
Philip the Good, firmly on the English side. Queen Isabella and
the city of Paris followed suit, with the result that there was
concluded the Treaty of Troyes (1420), whereby Henry became
Regent and Heir of France, marrying also Catherine, charming
daughter of Charles VI. The great northern block of Brittany,
Normandy, Maine and Champagne – together with Guyenne in
the far South West – were in English hands when Henry died in
August 1422. Charles VI's existence dragged on for seven more
miserable weeks. When death released him on 21 October the
infant Henry VI of England was proclaimed his successor.

Charles VII, by J. Fouquet 1425–1480

*(Louvre, Paris. Photo Giraudon)*

# CHARLES VII, 1422–1461
## (Son of CHARLES VI and Isabella of Bavaria)

Born 1403, was 19 when he ascended the throne, and 58 when he died.

Married Mary of Anjou and had sixteen children, including:
> LOUIS XI
> Catherine – married Charles the Bold, Duke of Burgundy
> Yolande – married Amadeus IX, Duke of Savoy
> Joan – married John, Duke of Bourbon
> Madeleine – married Gaston of Foix, Prince of Viane
> Charles, Duke of Berry and Guyenne

*Thumbnail Sketch* Weak in body and in character, deeply pious but of dubious morality, this monarch (possibly aided by his Queen and his mistress Agnes Sorel) eventually developed a capacity for using able subordinates.

### WHAT TO KNOW

The reign of Charles VII, destined to be a great one, opened in misery and shame. Henry VI's uncle, the Duke of Bedford, strong in his alliance with Philip the Good of Burgundy, prosecuted the war relentlessly and successfully. By 1429 the feeble sway of the King of France extended over slightly more territory than was controlled by Marshal Pétain in 1940 – that is to say the area beyond the Loire, with the exception of the western strip of Guyenne and Gascony. The wretched monarch, gyrating like a weathercock amongst his incompetent favourites, showed no capacity for defending, let alone exploiting, this compact geographical block, and it seemed that nothing could stop the invaders eliminating his "Kingdom of Bourges", as it was ironically styled after its capital. With this end in view they sought to establish a bridge-head and laid siege to Orleans.

It is a relief, amidst what Voltaire called "the crimes, follies and miseries" of history, to come upon a moment of unimpeachable nobility. Joan of Arc, a seventeen-year-old country girl from Domrémy in Lorraine, now, in 1429, appeared to save France. Familiarity can breed no contempt for the religious enthusiasm, high courage, psychological insight and sound common sense which characterize her story: the persuasion of Baudricourt (in command at Vaucouleurs), the journey to Chinon, the recognition of Charles, the relief of Orleans, the victory of Patay, the taking of Troyes, the coronation at Rheims, the failure before Paris, the capture at Compiègne by the Burgundians, the sale to the English, the propaganda trial at Rouen and the flickering faggots in the market square on 30 May 1431. Saint Joan, like all great leaders, expressed feelings which lie deep in the hearts of the inarticulate masses. She did more than defeat the English. She created French patriotism.

The tide now ran for France. Charles found a new confidence. The ceremony at Rheims had been fortifying to one who even doubted his own legitimacy – a fear not unreasonable for the child of Isabella of Bavaria. Through territorial and other concessions he achieved temporary reconciliation with Philip the Good of Burgundy (Treaty of Arras 1435), a grave blow to the English, who were further weakened by the death of the Duke of Bedford in the same year. In 1436 Paris welcomed Charles, and enemy activity became desultory enough to give France a breathing space for rehabilitation. Well served by a powerful council of able middle-class men, of whom Jacques Coeur – merchant, industrialist and financial adviser – and the brothers Bureau – fathers of

the formidable French artillery – are typical examples, the King undertook fiscal and military reforms. By the Pragmatic Sanction of Bourges (1438) the Church in France asserted a degree of independence from Rome – the attitude called "Gallicanism" – and the French economy was assisted by a considerable reduction in payments to the Papal treasury. But the great nobles, assisted by the Dauphin (later Louis XI), resenting the limitations placed on their activities by this alliance of monarch and bourgeoisie, indulged in a revolt which, because of its alleged similarity to the risings of the Hussites in Bohemia, was called the *Praguerie*. It

Altar frontal, about 1425
*(Victoria and Albert Museum. Crown Copyright)*

was swiftly suppressed and France's new standing army could now be turned against the English.

Apart from the period of the Truce of Tours (1444 to 1446), during which time Margaret of Anjou was married to Henry VI, hostilities proceeded steadily. (Margaret was daughter of that engaging Count of Provence whose appellation "Good King René" frequently mystifies travellers in those parts. He was also Duke of Anjou and Bar, and titular King of Naples, Sicily and Jerusalem.) By 1453 the English had lost everything except Calais and the Channel Islands. The Hundred Years War was over.

The reign, which started disastrously, ended sadly in July 1461. Charles had spent his last days at odds with the Dauphin (who fled to Burgundy) and in morbid fear of death by poison. But much had been achieved: national self-consciousness, expulsion of the foreigner, a strengthened monarchy, a decline in the power of the Estates, both General and Provincial, a powerful army and economic revival.

Louis XI
*(Burgundian School) (Mansell Collection)*

# LOUIS XI, 1461–1483

(Son of CHARLES VII and Mary of Anjou)

Born 1423, was 38 when he ascended the throne, and 60 when he died.

Married Margaret, daughter of James I of Scotland. No issue.

Married Charlotte of Savoy, and had seven children, including:

> Anne – married Peter of Beaujeu
>
> Joan (canonized 1950) – married LOUIS XII
>
> CHARLES VIII

*Thumbnail Sketch* Cynical, yet superstitious – this spider-like individual applied bourgeois business principles to the game of power politics and showed himself a Machiavellian before Machiavelli. The first French monarch to bear the title "Most Christian King".

## WHAT TO KNOW

When Louis XI was crowned at least one Frenchman rejoiced, for François Villon, thirty-year-old poetic genius, was amongst those released from prison in celebration of the occasion. But many viewed this ruler with distaste. The Burgundians, whose guest he had been, looked vainly for rewards, the clergy resented his revocation of the Pragmatic Sanction of Bourges, while the nobility saw in his predilection for ministers of low degree and for mercenary soldiers threats to feudalism and chivalry. Powerful aristocrats including the Duke of Berry (the King's brother), the Duke of Brittany and Charles the Bold, Count of Charolais (heir to Philip the Good of Burgundy), formed the "League of the Public Weal" against Louis who, after some indecisive fighting (Montlhéry 1465), weathered the storm by reason of support from the citizens of Paris and a policy of temporary appeasement (treaties of Conflans and Saint Maur, 1465).

Indeed, this great reign started unpromisingly and provides a story of almost continual struggle. The leader of successive leagues against the King was Charles the Bold, whose soaring ambitions give the clue to the complicated and turbulent proceedings.

The rise of the Burgundian power had been a factor of great significance in the history of France since John the Good gave the duchy to his son Philip the Bold in 1363 (see page 85). There had been four Great Dukes: Philip the Bold (1363–1404), John the Fearless (1404–1419), Philip the Good (1419–1467), and now there was Charles the Bold (1467–1477). Between them they had acquired territory which, with one major gap, extended from Holland in the North to the frontier of Savoy in the South. The gap was formed by the province of Champagne and the Duchy of Lorraine. It was particularly on Lorraine, and – indeed – on the Swiss cantons, that Charles cast an expansionist eye. He envisaged a revival of Lothair's ninth-century Middle Kingdom stretching from the North Sea to the Mediterranean. Here, then, lay the root of the troubles.

The years 1467–1477 passed in hostilities and intrigues. In 1475 Edward IV of England came to the aid of his brother-in-law Charles (the Duke had married Edward's sister Margaret in 1468) but was characteristically bought off by Louis at the Treaty of Pecquigny. In the same year Charles scored an important success in the conquest of Lorraine, but the Swiss, seeing their own independence threatened, took the offensive and defeated him at Grandson and Morat in 1476. In 1477 this last of the medieval knights met his end before Nancy.* The great Burgundian project collapsed.

Charles' possessions of Artois, Picardy and Burgundy now reverted to Louis XI, but it was a blow for France when Charles' only daughter, Mary, destined by Louis for the Dauphin, took the remaining lands to the Hapsburgs by marrying, in 1477, Maximilian of Austria, who became Holy Roman Emperor in 1493. This match was of

* *The Cross of Lorraine*
The double-barred Cross of Lorraine is of ancient origin. The top bar represents the title written by Pilate and set up over the head of Christ. This cross became popular in the Duchy of Lorraine as the result of its use at the battle of Nancy (1477), was later associated with the cult of Joan of Arc, was adopted as a symbol of hope after 1870 and became the natural sign of resistance to the heathen swastika in 1940.

The Burleigh Nef, silver gilt, 1482–1483
*(Victoria and Albert Museum. Crown Copyright)*

supreme importance in that from it was born Philip, who would marry Joanna of Spain in 1496, and become father of the Emperor Charles V. In the future, France was to feel herself menaced by the encircling power of the Austro-Spanish house.

Other territorial gains of Louis XI's reign included Cerdagne and Roussillon (1473), and, after the death of "good King René" and his nephew (1480, 1481), Maine, Anjou and Provence. This made France better knit and, as Louis continued to assert his authority over the nobility, a more formidable power unit than she had been in 1461.

The reign saw, too, the development of industry, commerce and communications, the installation of the first French printing press (1469) and the work of her first modern historian (and important source for this period), Philip de Commines. Louis had no desire to quit the scene of his success. He spent his last years at Plessis-lez-Tours, which he built, surrounded by elaborate security precautions, enlisting the aids of religious superstition and medical science in order that his life might be prolonged. Death came to him, however, on 30 August, 1483.

Charles VIII, after Le Maître de Charles VIII. End fifteenth century

*( Musée Condé, Chantilly. Photo Giraudon )*

# CHARLES VIII, 1483–1498

## (Son of LOUIS XI and Charlotte of Savoy)

Born 1470, was 13 when he ascended the throne, and 28 when he died.

Married Anne of Brittany, but his four children predeceased him.

*Thumbnail Sketch*   Weak in body, underdeveloped in mind – but of courageous and kindly disposition – this monarch was ambitious for power and its trappings. Love of adventure dictated his policies.

## WHAT TO KNOW

Louis XI despised his son, but, though his assessment of feminine mental equipment was normally unenthusiastic, regarded his competent twenty-two-year-old daughter, Anne of Beaujeu, as "the least silly woman in France". So it was decided that Charles VIII should start his reign in the care of his sister and her husband Peter of Beaujeu.

Anne – "Madame La Grande" – determined to maintain the autocratic tradition of her father. She rapidly dismissed the Estates General of 1484 and crushed the noble revolts ("the Crazy War") in which the King's cousin and eventual successor, Louis, Duke of Orleans and Duke Francis II of Brittany were concerned (1485–1488). Francis promised that his heiress, Anne of Brittany, should not be married without the permission of the King of France, but hardly had he died (1488) when complicated matrimonial problems arose. Charles VIII had been betrothed for four years to the enchanting Margaret, daughter of Maximilian of Austria. Maximilian, whose first wife, Mary of Burgundy, had died in 1482, now coveted Brittany, and married the Duchess Anne secretly, by proxy and without the French King's leave in 1490. The threat of encirclement to France was intolerable and reaction inevitably immediate. The King led a formidable army into Brittany to court the Duchess himself, the eleven-year-old Margaret was returned to her father, and, in 1491, the wedding of Charles and Anne took place at Rennes. It was argued that the proxy marriage with Maximilian was invalid, as having been contracted without Charles' consent, and the assimilation to the Royal domain of the great Breton fief was assured. Curiously enough the unprepossessing King and Duchess fell in love, and, on all grounds, the Regent could now retire with a sense of work well done.

Charles coped briskly with the aftermath of this coup. Menaced by Maximilian from the North, by Henry VII of England from the West and Ferdinand of Spain from the South, he satisfied the first by ceding Artois and Franche Comté, bought off the second at the Treaty of Etaples and pacified the third with Cerdagne and Roussillon. The curtain now rose on his great adventure.

Contemporary Italy presented a fascinating objective for aggression. Art, learning, wealth and luxury went hand in hand with corruption, political division and military incompetence. Louis XI had inherited the ancient Angevin claim to Naples and Sicily, now held by a bastard of the House of Aragon. Ludovico Sforza of Milan, and others, had their own reasons for inviting Charles VIII to make good this claim. The young monarch, inspired by an anachronistic conception of chivalry and bogus crusading zeal, swept his fine army through the peninsula to enter flower-strewn Naples, seeing in this easy triumph a step towards Constantinople and Jerusalem. But Europe could not acquiesce in such French aggrandizement. The League of

Venice, comprising various Italian states, together with Ferdinand of Aragon, Maximilian of Austria and Henry VII of England, was formed behind Charles, who was forced to retrace his steps and fight his way out of Italy at the battle of Fornovo (1495).

A number of Frenchmen thus brought into contact with Renaissance Italy returned with new ideas – at any rate about riches and comfort. Such conceptions had already been infiltrating unobtrusively, and were stimulated by the sightseeing element of this *promenade militaire*. Highly significant, however, is

Cupboard. Reign of Charles VIII
*(Victoria and Albert Museum. Crown Copyright)*

the coalition rapidly formed against the aggressor and the start of
a long Franco-Spanish rivalry.

Charles now devoted himself, for a space, to the welfare of
France, though Italy was clearly seldom absent from his thoughts.
Italians beautified Amboise, his birth-place, where, on 7 April
1498, he died, having crashed his head on the lintel of a low
doorway as he led his Queen to observe the innocent diversion of a
tennis match.

Louis XII
*(Bibliothèque Nationale, Estampes, Paris)*

# LOUIS XII, 1498–1515

(Son of Charles, Duke of Orleans and Mary of Cleves, great
  grandson of CHARLES V, cousin of CHARLES VIII.)

Born 1462, was 35 when he ascended the throne, and 52 when he
died.

Married Joan of France, daughter of Louis XI, but had no
  children. Marriage annulled 1498.

Married Anne of Brittany – had two sons who died young and two
  daughters, of whom
      Claude married Francis of Angoulême, later FRANCIS I

Married Mary of England, sister of Henry VIII, but had no
  children.


*Thumbnail Sketch*   Benevolent and generous at home – but ruthless and unintelligent in the pursuit of a disastrous foreign policy.


## WHAT TO KNOW

Louis XII, whose treason during the previous reign had earned
him imprisonment at Bourges, swiftly relieved many apprehensive
persons by observing that "the King of France does not avenge
the wrongs of the Duke of Orleans". An adventurous, if unwise,
foreign policy was foreshadowed when, at his coronation, he not
only assumed Charles VIII's titles of King of France, Jerusalem
and the two Sicilies, but arrogated to himself Milan, claimed
through his grandmother, Valentina Visconti (see page 87). But
it was necessary to secure the home front before undertaking forays
abroad. The new monarch wished to discard the unattractive and
childless wife forced upon him by Louis XI. He also desired the
widowed Anne of Brittany, on personal grounds and in order to
ensure that her duchy did not regain its independence. Pope
Alexander VI was ready to oblige with a dispensation, and the
glad news was carried to Chinon by his son Caesar Borgia, who was
rewarded with a bride, a fine dowry and the Dukedom of
Valentinois.

  Encouraged by the Borgias, who hoped to promote their
policies; supported by the Venetians, who desired the discomfiture

of Milan; pushed on by his minister – George of Amboise, Arch-bishop of Rouen – who wished to become Pope; allied with Savoy, ready to offer passage to French troops, and impelled by his own inclinations, Louis descended upon Italy in 1499. Milan fell and remained under his rule for twelve years. An attempted comeback by Ludovico Sforza resulted in the latter's capture and barbarous imprisonment at Loches until his death in 1508. It was now the turn of Naples.

This kingdom, clearly, could not be annexed without offending Spain, both on dynastic grounds and because Ferdinand of Aragon looked to it for a significant proportion of his corn supply. The two monarchs hit upon the happy solution of partition (Treaty of Granada, 1500) and next year the French marched south. Naples fell, but Franco-Spanish co-operation broke down. By December 1503, defeated at Garigliano by their late ally, the French abandoned this Neapolitan venture.

There followed foreign political negotiations of incredible ineptitude. Anne of Brittany, having failed to give Louis a son, was unwilling that their daughter Claude should marry the heir presumptive, Francis of Angoulême. For this reason, and to gain the Imperial favour, Claude had been affianced to Charles, grandson of the Emperor Maximilian, and destined to be the Emperor Charles V. This arrangement was now confirmed by the Treaty of Blois (1504), where Maximilian's recognition of Louis as Duke of Milan was dearly bought with Claude's promised eventual dowry of Brittany, Burgundy, Milan and Genoa. Such spoliation of France, however, was un-acceptable, and, in 1506, the Estates General at Tours persuaded a willing monarch to reverse his decision. Thus Claude married Angoulême in 1514.

Louis XII would now have done well to rest content, but he joined the League of Cambrai (1508) whereby he, the Emperor, Pope Julius II, and Ferdinand of Aragon proposed to plunder Venice. The Venetians, defeated by the French at Agnadello (1509),

Triptych. Limoges enamel. *c.* 1500
*( Victoria and Albert Museum. Crown Copyright)*

withdrew behind their natural defences and, after a space, the warrior Pope changed his tune. His Holy League (1511) purposed to drive the barbarous foreigner Louis XII from Italy. The Emperor, Spain, Venice, England and the Swiss were eager to assist. Louis likened himself humorously to the infidel Turk. A French victory at Ravenna (1512) was offset by defeat at Novara (1513) and by 1514 another Italian incident was closed and peace made. Great captains: La Tremouille, the brilliant Gaston de Foix and Bayard, *"le chevalier sans peur et sans reproche"*, had struggled valiantly but ineffectively. All that had been gained was lost.

But France did not suffer internally from these hostilities. Agriculture prospered, taxation was lightened, justice done. The population increased, advancing civilization showed itself at Chaumont, Blois and elsewhere. Louis was hailed as *"Pater Patriae"*. Widowed in 1514, but adventurous still, he now married Mary of England, lovely sister of Henry VIII. The bride submitted, with the guarantee that, on her husband's demise, she would be permitted to make a love match. Her wish was granted. Exhausted by this final effort Louis XII died on 1 January 1515.

# RENAISSANCE
## 1515–1589

| | |
|---|---|
| Francis I | 1515–1547 |
| Henry II | 1547–1559 |
| Francis II | 1559–1560 |
| Charles IX | 1560–1574 |
| Henry III | 1574–1589 |

*(In England cf. TUDOR 1485–1558;*
*ELIZABETHAN 1558–1603)*

| | |
|---|---|
| Henry VIII | 1509–1547 |
| Edward VI | 1547–1553 |
| Mary | 1553–1558 |
| Elizabeth I | 1558–1603 |

RENAISSANCE
Pavilion of Henry II. The Louvre, Paris

# RENAISSANCE
## 1515–1589

The accession of Francis I makes a convenient and not entirely unconvincing starting point for Renaissance architecture in France, though Italian influence had been at work (e.g. the Normandy château of Gaillon) before 1515. Campaigners from 1494 onwards had brought back from Italy a taste for wealth and luxury and, with their return, there started an early French Renaissance period (roughly Francis I's first fifteen years) during which we find native medievalism decorated with the finery of a foreign revival of the antique. The result is a mixture – observe it, as you travel down the Loire, making (amongst many pauses) visits to Chambord, Blois, Chenonceaux and Azay-le-Rideau. Just as at Compton Wynyates you will find a hint of anachronistic fortification, so here are examples of the essentially inoffensive defensive. Towers rise from which no culverin could ever bang, turrets taper up from which no crossbowman would discharge his bolt. It is, rather, the day of the cherub, the arabesque, the baluster and the cornucopia. As the century continues, architecture undergoes a later Renaissance – the result of Italian study-journeys by French architects (e.g. Jean Bullant and Philibert Delorme), of the employment of Italian artists in France: Serlio (chiefly important for his influential treatise on architecture), Rosso and Primaticcio (particularly associated with Fontainebleau), and of learned publications dealing with classical antiquity. The following of ancient models is now infinitely more scholarly, though the indigenous high pitched roofs and dormer windows remain – ingeniously combined with principles derived from Greece and Rome. Triumphs are achieved in the construction of Pierre Lescot's superb façade in the Cour Carrée of the Louvre (1549–1556) and in the Tuileries, commissioned by Catherine de' Medici in 1563, just before the wars of religion effectively slowed down the rate of building.

Francis I, with his wife
(Franco-Flemish School)

# FRANCIS I, 1515–1547

(Son of Charles, Count of Angoulême and Louise of Savoy;
great-great-grandson of CHARLES V, cousin and son-in-law of
LOUIS XII)

Born 1494, was 20 when he ascended the throne, and 52 when he
died.

Married Claude of France, daughter of LOUIS XII, by whom he
had eight children including:

> HENRY II
>
> Charles, Duke of Orleans – died 1545
>
> Madeleine – married James V of Scotland in 1537 and
> died the same year
>
> Margaret – married Emmanuel Philibert of Savoy

Married Eleanor of Portugal, sister of Emperor Charles V. No
issue.

*Thumbnail Sketch*   Impressively handsome, enormously vigorous
over a wide range of activities, abounding in culture, panache and
sensuality, this ambitious but essentially superficial despot "was
unconsciously the champion of a great cause". (G. W. Kitchin,
*A History of France.*)

## WHAT TO KNOW

"That big fellow will spoil everything," said Louis XII of his
successor, and Francis I certainly took risks. The frivolous fas-
cination of Italy persisted, driving him across the Alps in 1515 to
victory at Marignano over the papally employed Swiss, and to
knighthood – conferred by Bayard. Francis held Milan until 1521,
concluded the "Perpetual Peace" of Freiburg (1516) with his
adversaries, (whereby Swiss mercenaries served French monarchs
until the reign of Louis XVI), and made an agreement with
Pope Leo X which was to last for the same period. By this
Concordat of Bologna (1516) the authority of the Holy See was
deemed superior to that of a General Council, the payment of
certain financial dues to Rome was revived, while the Supreme
Pontiff permitted the royal nomination of French bishops, subject
to ecclesiastical investiture by himself. This nomination power
was to prove valuable to French Kings in withstanding the later
reforming assaults of Luther and Calvin.

On 11 January 1519 there occurred an event of European magnitude in the death of the Emperor Maximilian. His grandson, already Charles I of Spain, now disposed of the Netherlands, Flanders, Artois, Franche-Comté, Austria, Naples, Sicily, Sardinia, Aragon, Castile and Spanish South America. On 28 June this nineteen-year-old Hapsburg was elected Holy Roman Emperor, as Charles V, despite the competition of Francis I and Henry VIII of England. The concentration of territory and power was phenomenal. Would this Colossus crush the growing life out of France? Would France – wealthy, bellicose and by now a formidable geographical block – upset the equilibrium of these dispersed dominions? The stage was set for a conflict during which Henry VIII threw his weight first on one side, then on the other, a policy forecast by his meetings with Francis at the Field of Cloth of Gold – and with Charles at Canterbury and Gravelines, in 1520.

Francis and Charles did, in fact, engage in four wars between 1521 and 1544. The Low Countries, Italy and France suffered hostilities. The Constable of Bourbon, a great French feudatory, betrayed his King (thus permitting the latter to annex valuable estates); Bayard was killed; Francis was captured at Pavia (1525) and, while imprisoned, signed the humiliating Treaty of Madrid – understandably repudiating it on being set at liberty. War and peace alternated. In 1530 Francis married the Emperor's sister; 1539 saw him offering sumptuous entertainment to his brother-in-law; on other occasions, as necessity dictated, "Most Christian France" allied itself with German protestants and with Sultan Solyman the Magnificent against the Emperor. By the Peace of Crespy (1544) – a relief to both monarchs – Francis' sacrifice of feudal lordship over Artois and Flanders was compensated by Charles' renunciation of Burgundy, while the French abandonment of the Neapolitan claim, followed, in the next year, by Charles' investiture of his son Philip with the Duchy of Milan,

Part of a plaque. Limoges enamel. Representing St. Thomas,
with the features of Francis I. (L. Limosin)
*(Louvre, Paris. Photo des Musées Nationaux)*

settled the Hapsburg grip on Italy until the late eighteenth
century. France had opposed a vast power, and kept herself in
being; but the Gallo-Teutonic struggle, destined to bedevil
European history for more than four hundred years, had been
initiated.

At home this was the reign of an absolutist, characterized by
increased centralization and a brilliant court, where an élite
amongst the nobility followed the precepts of Baldassare Cas-
tiglione's "The Courtier". Renaissance splendour developed
apace at Amboise (Leonardo da Vinci died nearby in 1519),
Blois, Chambord, Saint-Germain-en-Laye, the Louvre, and, above
all, at Fontainebleau where Rosso and Primaticcio beautified the
palace in which Benvenuto Cellini worked. The Collège de
France was founded in 1531, Rabelais produced *"Pantagruel"*
in 1533 and *"Gargantua"* in 1535, Francis' brilliant and charming
sister, Margaret of Navarre, patronized men of letters like
Clément Marot and endeavoured to protect reformers in religion.
Luther made his protest at Wittenberg in 1517, Lefèvre d'Etaples
published the New Testament in French in 1523, Calvin was
established at Geneva in 1536. In this matter of religious reform
Francis blew hot and cold, but there *was* persecution – one recalls
the massacre of the Vaudois heretics in Provence in 1545. The
latter half of the century would see religious wars.

Francis died at Rambouillet on 31 March 1547, worn out by a
reign of which the vast energy, if sometimes misdirected, is not to
be denied.

Henry II, by François Clouet 1516–1572

*(Musée Condé, Chantilly. Photo Giraudon)*

# HENRY II, 1547–1559
## (Son of FRANCIS I and Claude of France)

Born 1519, was 28 when he ascended the throne, and 40 when he was killed.

Married Catherine de' Medici, by whom he had ten children including:

> FRANCIS II
> CHARLES IX
> HENRY III
> Francis, Duke of Alençon and Anjou (died 1584)
> Elizabeth – married Philip II of Spain
> Margaret – married HENRY IV

*Thumbnail Sketch* Gloomy, taciturn, cold and a Catholic bigot – this monarch possessed the vigour and courage of Francis I, without his sparkle. He was, however, probably superior in judgement.

## WHAT TO KNOW

Amongst those who hovered influentially near the throne of Henry II were Diana of Poitiers and two Guise brothers. Diana of Poitiers, Duchess of Valentinois, was a chilly, imperious, intelligent beauty twenty years Henry's senior. Captivated when Dauphin, he loved her till he died. Concurrently the Guise star rose. This family was a cadet branch of the ducal house of Lorraine. One of its members, Claude, was created first Duke of Guise by Francis I. He assisted the Queen Mother, Louise of Savoy, during her regency when Francis was a prisoner in Madrid. Claude's sons – Duke Francis and Charles, Cardinal of Lorraine, played important roles under Henry II, while their sister Mary, second wife of James V of Scotland, was mother of Mary, Queen of Scots. In the background was an able Queen, Catherine de' Medici, preoccupied, for the nonce, with childbirth.

Henry II was immediately involved in war with England. In 1547 Protector Somerset invaded Scotland to woo the infant Mary Stuart for the child Edward VI. France, fearing the union of these crowns, aided the Scots and spirited away the little Queen to betrothal with the Dauphin Francis, delighting the Guises

who thus remained powerful in Edinburgh and on the Loire.
Peace was made in 1550, France having recovered Boulogne. Two
years later Henry gladly allied himself with certain German
Protestant Princes against his father's old enemy the Emperor
Charles V and occupied Verdun, Metz and Toul at their invita-
tion. Militarily he was looking in the right direction and it was a
blessing for France when the Religious Peace of Augsburg (1555)
shattered Charles V's dream of a united Germany and drove the
Emperor to abdication. The next Emperor was Ferdinand I,
Charles' brother (Archduke of Austria, King of Hungary and
Bohemia), while Charles' son, Philip II (married to Mary Tudor)
inherited Spain, the Netherlands, Franche-Comté, Naples and
Spanish America. The Truce of Vaucelles (1556) sensibly guaranteed five years Franco-Spanish peace, but was immediately
broken when the Neapolitan Pope Paul IV suggested that Henry
should free Naples from Spain. Guise marched South and was
defeated by the Duke of Alva. In the North, Coligny saved Paris
by prolonging the defence of St. Quentin – a relieving force under
Montmorency being routed -- and Guise retrieved his reputation
by the brilliant capture of Calais (1558), England's last foothold in
France. By the Peace of Cateau Cambrésis France restored Savoy
and Piedmont to the Duke of Savoy (who married Henry's sister
Margaret), but retained Calais, Verdun, Metz and Toul. Henry's
daughter Elizabeth married the widowed Philip II of Spain.

Within France artistic and architectural activity
continued. Ronsard, Du Bellay and other poets
of the *Pléiade* brought classical standards and
new elegance to French poetry – but many
minds were captured by the sombre, logical
doctrines now pouring from Calvin's
Geneva. Protestant communities, with a
republican flavour pleasing to indepen-
dent-minded nobles, were widespread,
despite sharp persecution. Religious
war was becoming inevitable. Such was
the situation when Henry, jousting with
Montgomery, Captain of his Scottish
Guard, at the marriage celebrations

Diane de Poitiers (François Clouet 1516–1572)
*(National Gallery of Art, Washington D.C. Samuel H. Kress Collection)*

of Elizabeth and Philip II, was pierced in the eye and killed on
10 July 1559.

Francis II, by François Clouet 1516–1572

*(Bibliothèque Nationale, Paris. Photo Giraudon)*

# FRANCIS II, 1559–1560

### (Son of HENRY II and Catherine de' Medici)

Born 1544, was 15 when he ascended the throne, and 16 when he died.

Married Mary Stuart (Mary, Queen of Scots) and had no children.

*Thumbnail Sketch*   This bilious adolescent passed his short reign in the arms of Mary Stuart and the pocket of the Guises.

## WHAT TO KNOW

Henry II's death spelt gloom and crisis for France. The sickly boy who now succeeded to the throne adored his girl-wife, Mary Stuart, and accepted submissively the domination of her Guise uncles, Duke Francis and the Cardinal – "the brood of false Lorraine". Diana of Poitiers was bustled out of lovely Chenonceaux by Catherine de' Medici and, though offered Chaumont, withdrew to Anet and died in 1566. Montmorency, a prisoner of war from the battle of St. Quentin until the peace of Cateau Cambrésis, returned to a chilly reception. The Guises, now increased in grandeur by an unconvincing claim to descent from Charlemagne, tightened their grip upon the levers of power.

But these fierce protagonists of militant catholicism, bent on pursuing the persecution policy of the latter years of the previous reign, were not without opponents. The Bourbon family, who traced their ancestry back to Robert of Clermont, youngest son of Saint Louis (see page 55), were represented by the vacillating Antony of Bourbon, King of Navarre, and, more formidably, by his younger brother Louis, Prince of Condé, an able soldier whose Protestantism was doubtless strengthened by the disregard in which his distinguished services had been held by a jealous catholic court. Other important Huguenots, as the members of the reformed church in France came to be called (the word derives from the German *Eidgenossen* – persons bound together by an oath) were Montmorency's nephews, prominent amongst whom was the famous Admiral Gaspard de Coligny. And, scattered throughout the land, were people who, encouraged by the example of their co-religionists in Scotland, England and the Netherlands, were prepared, if need be, to fight for the new faith.

The Guises were not slow to provide provocation. On 23 December 1559 a Counsellor of the Parliament of Paris, improbably named Anne du Bourg, whose opinions had been pronounced heretical, was burned on the Place de Grève. A plot to avenge him, by the overthrow of the Lorrainers, was soon on foot – with an obscure leader called La Renaudie, who, doubtless, had influential sponsors behind him. The Guise intelligence got wind of La Renaudie's intentions, the court was moved from Blois to the stronghold of Amboise, where the malcontents received a rough reception and the young royal couple were able to enjoy the spectacle of their prisoners dangling from the battlements and drowning in the Loire. Such was the Conspiracy or Tumult of Amboise, by which "coming events cast their shadows before".

But, for the moment, wiser policies prevailed. Catherine de' Medici, an intelligent and sensible politician who believed that religious difficulties could be resolved by conference, in a spirit of reason, compromise and reconciliation, achieved the appointment of Michel de l'Hôpital, a highly experienced and much travelled lawyer, as Chancellor of France. An Assembly of Notables was convened at Fontainebleau, the hand of persecution was temporarily stayed, and the Estates General were called for the end

Great Seal of Francis II and Mary Stuart, 1559
*(Service Photographique des Archives Nationales)*

of the year – enlightened steps which in no way accorded with the sinister designs of the heretic-hunting Guises. At their instance, when the Estates General met at Orléans, Condé was arrested and condemned to death before a special court. But hardly had this verdict been obtained when it became apparent that the Guises' tool, the King, was desperately ill with the ear trouble which continually afflicted him. Duke Francis sought to stimulate the doctors with threats, the Cardinal of Lorraine mobilized the resources of the church and called the faithful to prayer – but the King died on 5 December 1560 and Condé was saved.

Charles IX, attributed to François Clouet 1516–1572

*(Musée Condé, Chantilly. Photo Giraudon)*

# CHARLES IX, 1560–1574
## (Son of HENRY II and Catherine de' Medici, brother of FRANCIS II)

Born 1550, was 10 when he ascended the throne, and 23 when he died.

Married Elizabeth of Austria, daughter of Emperor Maximilian II, by whom he had one daughter, who died young.

*Thumbnail Sketch* A weak, idle, sensitive, not unattractive boy who suffered from tuberculosis, hallucinations, an immoderate passion for hunting, and a subtly dominating mother.

## WHAT TO KNOW

The accession of Charles IX, a malleable child, gave a long-awaited opportunity to his mother Catherine de' Medici. This typical product of the Italian renaissance stuck at nothing in what was to prove an unsuccessful attempt to achieve her objects: the acquisition of power for herself and the preservation of absolute monarchy for her children in a unified and peaceful France. Her policy as Regent was that of balance between warring factions — with, for the moment, the scales tilted in favour of the Bourbons rather than the Guises, whose niece, Mary Stuart, was now dispatched to Scotland. The Chancellor, Michel de l'Hôpital, urged Christian unity upon the Estates General, but an uneasy conference between Catholics and Protestants at Poissy broke down, though the famous "Edict of January" 1562 permitted certain Huguenot religious services.

However, the compromise argued in the Council Chamber awoke no echo in men's hearts — throughout France there was bickering and iconoclasm. Eventually the first of nine consecutive civil wars broke out when, on 1 March 1562, the adherents of Duke Francis of Guise, following their master through the town of Vassy in Champagne, slaughtered some Huguenots assembled for illegal hymn-singing. Catholics led by the Guises, and Protestants under Condé, now sprang to arms. Aid was sought on the one hand from Spain, stronghold of the old faith, and, on the other, from Elizabeth I of England and heretical German princes.

Antony of Bourbon, the Protestant leader who had defected to the Catholics, fell before Rouen; his brother Condé was captured at Dreux; the Duke of Guise was shot near Orléans – and peace, for a few years, was achieved by the Edict of Amboise (1563). But the story, with variations, was to be repeated again and again. Only an immensely powerful hand could have imposed peace upon the France of the second half of the sixteenth century – and that, the hand of Henry of Navarre, was not to be available until 1589.

As it was the reign saw three more civil wars, each with its own settlement. Great figures passed: Condé at Jarnac in 1569, Michel de l'Hôpital in 1573. Huguenot power increased, and the growing King began to resent maternal domination, now relying on Admiral de Coligny, Condé's successor as Protestant leader. Such a situation was intolerable to the jealous Catherine, the more so since new policies were shaped of which she disapproved. Admittedly she had engineered Charles' marriage with Elizabeth of Austria, daughter of the tolerant Emperor Maximilian II; she was happy that two religions should lie in one bed by reason of the union of her daughter Margaret of Valois and Henry of Navarre (nineteen-year-old Huguenot figurehead, son of Antony of Bourbon), and there was the consideration of Elizabeth of England for her youngest son. But the Coligny conception that Frenchmen should find unity in an attack on Spain seemed to her folly dan-

gerous enough to justify the elimination of the admiral, an opinion in which young Duke Henry of Guise concurred, for he believed Coligny to have encompassed his father's death. The abortive attempt was made on 22 August 1572, in a Paris crowded with Huguenot aristocracy, up for the Margaret-Henry wedding. This failure led Catherine and her confederates to persuade the King that a Huguenot insurrection could only be averted by the execution of "those who intended to rise against the state". In the small hours of 24 August the church bell of Saint-Germain-l'Auxerrois signalled the massacre of Saint Bartholomew. Coligny

Helmet of Charles IX: gold enamelled
*(Louvre, Paris. Photo des Musées Nationaux)*

and many others fell and, of course, civil war flared again – to be concluded in 1573 with the usual amnesty, a further guarantee of freedom of conscience, and free public worship for Huguenots in the protestant cities of La Rochelle, Montauban and Nîmes. A glimmer of hope in a murky future lay in the rise of the *Politiques*, of whom de l'Hôpital is the prototype – a party valuing strong royal government more than religious faith. Little optimism, however, cheered the last days of the unhappy Charles IX who died, racked by nightmares and convulsions (aggravated, it has been suggested, by excessive efforts on his hunting horn), on 30 May 1574.

Henry III, artist unknown. Sixteenth century
*( Musée Condé, Chantilly. Photo Giraudon)*

# HENRY III, 1574–1589

(Son of HENRY II and Catherine de' Medici,
brother of FRANCIS II and CHARLES IX)

Born 1551, was 22 when he ascended the throne, and 38 when he
died.

Married Louise de Lorraine-Vaudémont, and had no children.

*Thumbnail Sketch*  This intelligent, fastidious and effeminate
monarch displayed "a strange compound of debauchery and
repentance, impiety and superstition" (Dumas), and was totally
incapable of commanding respect.

## WHAT TO KNOW

Henry of Valois, Duke of Anjou, had been elected King of
Poland in 1573 (Polish influence is to be detected in the later
ceremonial of Versailles), but, on learning of the death of his
brother Charles IX, was delighted to quit an exceedingly uncom-
fortable throne for that of France. He made a furtive exit from
Cracow, paused to divert himself in Italian resorts, and, shortly
after his return, allied himself with the Guises by marrying Louise
de Lorraine-Vaudémont. The likelihood of his begetting children
was, however, remote, and it was clear that the crown would go
eventually either to the fourth son of Henry II – Francis, Duke of
Alençon – or to Henry of Navarre, a situation which added com-
plication to a number of doubtful issues.

Four more civil wars were fought during this reign, in which
government was unsatisfactory to Catholics and Protestants alike.
The role of the *Politiques* increased in importance as they reached
agreement with the Huguenots and were joined by Alençon and
Navarre. In 1576 the "Peace of Monsieur" (from now on this
title was borne by the eldest brother of the King of France) gave
great concessions: the reformed worship was allowed openly,
except in Paris; arrangements were made to ensure justice for
Protestants in mixed legal cases; Huguenot forces might hold
eight strong places, and the Estates General were to meet. To
offset this (and taking advantage of the genuine fervour and grow-

ing force of the Counter-Reformation) Duke Henry of Guise formed the Holy League which, drawn from a wide variety of social strata, was as hostile to the monarchy as it was to Protestantism.

The Estates General, at Blois, were boycotted by the Huguenots. It became thus an all-Catholic body – which not only attacked heresy but also certain monarchical institutions. Henry sought to serve his own interests by embracing the Holy League and so, yet again, provoked civil war. It ended swiftly with the Peace of Bergerac (1577), only slightly less favourable to the reformed religion than had been the "Peace of Monsieur". At any rate, with the exception of a short burst of hostilities in 1579–1580, it lasted for seven years.

In 1584 Alençon, who had been courting Elizabeth of England and fishing in the troubled waters of the Netherlands' struggle against Spain, fell a victim to the consumption which had carried off many members of his house. The Huguenot Henry of Navarre, who could trace his descent through ten generations directly back to Saint Louis, now became heir presumptive – a situation greatly displeasing to Guise and the Holy League. Guise had designs on the French throne himself (did not his pedigree go back to Charlemagne?) and he straightway intrigued successfully for Spanish aid. He disposed of great strength in Paris and northern

France, but Navarre, who also counted on foreign assistance – from Denmark, the Elector Palatine and England – was powerful in the South West. Whither, between these two camps, was the King to turn? He opted for the Holy League, and, by the Treaty of Nemours (1585), withdrew the concessions made to his Protestant subjects. The result was the "War of the Three Henries" – Navarre, Guise and the monarch – two strong men and a bewildered shuttle-cock.

After approximately a year (1587–1588) of indecisive campaigning Henry of Guise entered Paris, against the express orders of the King, who immediately fled the capital

Bowl. Silver, parcel gilt. Second half of sixteenth century
*(Victoria and Albert Museum. Crown Copyright)*

he loved. He then bowed to the Holy League by the "Edict of Union" and summoned the Estates General to Blois. Guise joined him there, caused offence by his arrogance, and paid for it by falling victim to an assassination, perpetrated by members of Henry's "Forty-Five" Guard. This coup (23 December) did little to cheer the dying Catherine de' Medici and was followed, next day, by the murder of the Duke's Cardinal brother. However the Guise mantle fell on the surviving male member of the family, the Duke of Mayenne, who, backed by the League "Council of Sixteen" in Paris, assumed the title of "Lieutenant General of the State and crown of France". The King now turned to Henry of Navarre. Together, in the summer of 1589, they moved on Paris. An assault was planned, confidence reigned in the Royal headquarters at St. Cloud. But a feeble-minded Dominican friar named Jacques Clément penetrated to the presence, handed the monarch a document and stabbed him mortally. Dying, he exhorted those present to accept Navarre as his successor.

A note of cheer comes from the general area of Bordeaux. The exquisite essays of the great Montaigne were published between 1580 and 1588.

# CLASSICAL  Part 1
## 1589–1715

| | |
|---|---|
| Henry IV | 1589–1610 |
| Louis XIII | 1610–1643 |
| Louis XIV | 1643–1715 |

*(In England cf. ELIZABETHAN 1558–1603;*
*JACOBEAN 1603–1625; STUART 1625–1702;*
*GEORGIAN 1702–1830)*

| | |
|---|---|
| Elizabeth I | 1558–1603 |
| James I | 1603–1625 |
| Charles I | 1625–1649 |
| Commonwealth | 1649–1660 |
| Charles II | 1660–1685 |
| James II | 1685–1689 |
| William and Mary | 1689–1694 |
| William III | 1694–1702 |
| Anne | 1702–1714 |

CLASSICAL. Part 1
Château of Versailles. Western façade

(Photo Giraudon)

# CLASSICAL Part I
## 1589–1715

The seventeenth and eighteenth centuries, together with the epoch of the Consulate and the First Empire, may be regarded as constituting a period of classical architecture with variations. When Henry IV had pacified France, and the arts of peace revived, when the critical restraint of Malherbe prepared the way for Corneille and Racine, reverence for antique models increased an already existing respect for the Doric, Ionic and Corinthian orders. Churches in the severe so-called "Jesuit" style arose (e.g. that of the Sorbonne), François Mansart added the Gaston of Orleans wing to the château of Blois, Le Vau and Claude Perrault achieved the famous colonnade of the Louvre, and Jules Hardouin Mansart the great Church of the Dome at the Invalides. At almost the same time (1679) this talented architect stepped into the shoes of Louis Le Vau (1612–1670) and continued the latter's work on the château at Versailles. The great garden front (Le Vau and Mansart) expresses the spirit of a whole era in a style which is classical with a hint of baroque – perhaps best called "the style of Louis XIV" – epitomizing the authoritarianism and majesty of the Grand Siècle. The château of Versailles is also a memorial to the cultural dictatorship exercised by seventeenth- and eighteenth-century France over Europe. There would soon arise, from the Gulf of Finland to the Alps, palaces and houses with names such as Sans Souci, Monplaisir, Sans Pareil, Fantaisie and Monrepos – the polite world continued to pay its tribute to the Sun King long after that monarch's death in 1715.

Henry IV "amoureux"

*( Mansell Collection )*

# HENRY IV, 1589–1610

(Son of Antony of Bourbon and Jeanne d'Albret of Navarre,
direct descendant of LOUIS IX, distant cousin and
brother-in-law of HENRY III)

Born 1553, was 35 when he ascended the throne, and 56 when he
was assassinated.

Married Margaret of Valois by whom he had no children.
Marriage annulled 1599. Married Marie de' Medici and had
three sons (one died young):

> LOUIS XIII
> Gaston of Orleans

and three daughters:

> > Elizabeth – married Philip IV of Spain
> > Christine – married Victor Amadeus of Savoy
> > Henrietta Maria – married Charles I of England

*Thumbnail Sketch*  Gallant in battle and indefatigable in love
(56 mistresses, of whom Gabrielle d'Estrées and Henriette
d'Entragues are the most famous) Henry of Navarre combined
benevolence with ability and a genial contempt for his fellows. He
trod the path of absolutism naturally and with confidence.

## WHAT TO KNOW

The Capetian Valois were thus extinguished, but Capet blood
ran in the veins of Henry IV (whose mother sang a madrigal while
he was born!) – a Bourbon descended from Robert of Clermont,
sixth son of Saint Louis (see page 55). Married to Henry III's
sister, commended by that monarch as legitimate successor, this
Gascon Huguenot was not immediately acceptable to a land torn
by civil and religious war since 1562. Victories over the Catholic
League at Arques (1589) and Ivry (1590), followed by his states-
man-like renunciation of Protestantism, opened Paris to Henry
(1594) and made him ruler of France. War with Spain came in
1595 (Philip II had supported the League) and was concluded at
Vervins (1598), leaving Henry at last in a position to start his great
work of rehabilitation, bringing pacification, prosperity and power
to France.

Entrusting his soul's health to a Jesuit confessor and his physical well-being to a Huguenot doctor, Henry placed religious unity and peace high amongst his priorities. But his erstwhile co-religionists (1¼ million of them in a population of 15–20 millions) showed no inclination to follow their leader into the Roman fold, so an attempt was made to solve the problem by the Edict of Nantes (1598) which accorded to Protestants freedom of worship, unrestricted career opportunities, guaranteed justice and the right to maintain certain military strongholds. This act of toleration in an intolerant age, the triumph of the *Politiques*, permitted an *imperium in imperio* not without danger for France.

Prosperity returned as the result of joint efforts by Henry and his famous superintendent of finances, Sully. This dour Protestant bullied peculating officials into honest administration of an iniquitous fiscal system (the clergy and nobility remained exempt from direct taxation) and stimulated agriculture, the begetter of health, rural virtue, fecundity and cannon-fodder. In contrast, Henry, in order to prevent spending abroad, encouraged the luxury industries for which France became famous, and the whole development was facilitated by new roads and canals. The energy of the time was seen as far away as Quebec, founded by Champlain in 1608.

Henry, backed by the artillery gathered in Sully's arsenal, set

up as a counterpoise to the *Noblesse d'Epée* the *Noblesse de Robe* (a social category created by Sully's one original tax, *La Paulette*, payment of which rendered certain legal offices hereditary) and dominated his overmighty subjects by alternate exhibitions of charm and ruthlessness. Soon he could attack his foreign enemies – the Austrian Hapsburg Emperor and the Spanish Hapsburg King, who held him in a strategic straitjacket from the Netherlands to the Pyrenees. A campaign against Savoy won Bresse and Bugey (1600–1601), helping to ease this situation, but Henry was alarmed at the territorial gains which might

Chandelier of Marie de' Medici

*(Louvre, Paris. Photo des Musées Nationaux)*

accrue to the Emperor as a result of the disputed Cleves-Jülich succession and, in 1609, resolved to assail the Austro-Spanish foe. He was not without his critics at this time, but his assassination by Ravaillac (14 May 1610) in Paris, somewhere near No. 3 Rue de la Ferronnerie, assured to him a popularity which, boosted by Voltaire's *Henriade*, has survived to this day. We gaze upon the works he wrought in his capital, at Saint-Germain-en-Laye and Fontainebleau. To many he remains the monarch of *la poule au pot* and of the "snow-white plume", and romantics will always find a place in their hearts for their "Sovereign Lord, King Henry of Navarre".

Louis XIII as St. Louis,
by Philippe de Champaigne, French, 1602–1674. *c.* 1630
*(City Art Museum of Saint Louis, Missouri. Gift of Friends of the City Art Museum)*

# LOUIS XIII, 1610–1643
## (Son of HENRY IV and Marie de' Medici)

Born 1601, was 8 when he ascended the throne, and 48 when he died.

Married Anne of Austria, daughter of Philip III of Spain, and had two sons:

> LOUIS XIV
>
> Philip of Orleans – married (1) Henrietta of England, (2) Elizabeth Charlotte of the Palatinate

*Thumbnail Sketch* Intelligent, dutiful, pitiless and shy – this soldierly monarch, partnered and supported by Richelieu, governed France with authority.

## WHAT TO KNOW

The minority of Louis XIII necessitated a regency: Marie de' Medici and a council. Marie – stout, idle, stupid – was ruled by two disastrous Florentines: Concino Concini, created Marshal d'Ancre, and his wife Leonora Galigaï. A reversal of foreign policy withdrew France from the war against the Austro-Spanish house, and attempted to ally Bourbon and Hapsburg by the marriage of Louis XIII with Anne of Austria and of his sister Elizabeth with the Prince who would become Philip IV of Spain. At home the removal of Henry IV's strong hand necessitated the summons of the Estates General. They met in 1614 and were not to be called again until 1789. Their deliberations were abortive, but a great impression was made by the speech of a young bishop called Richelieu.

In 1617 Louis, weary of childish pursuits and the society of servants, took advice of his attractive falconer De Luynes, and seized power. Concini was shot; the Galigaï was burnt for witchcraft; Marie was exiled. De Luynes died during the ensuing turmoil with rebellious nobles and insurgent Huguenots, and the latter, retaining toleration, lost the right of political assembly and all their military strongholds except La Rochelle and Montauban. Reconciliation between the King and his mother was achieved by

Marie's protégé Richelieu (now Cardinal) who, at the instance of his patroness, entered the Royal Council in 1624.

Richelieu stated his objects clearly: "to ruin the Huguenot party, to bring down the pride of the nobles" and to raise the name of Louis XIII "among foreign nations to the honour that ought, of right, to belong to it".

In 1627 the Huguenots of La Rochelle rose, backed by that essentially amateur commander, the Duke of Buckingham. King and Cardinal (with Richelieu's remarkable "Grey Eminence", the Capucin Father Joseph, as Chief of Staff) besieged the city, which fell after loathsome privations. The Huguenots, losing all privileges except freedom of worship and careers, were pardoned by a master-stroke of policy, which finally stopped their separatist activities.

Aristocratic insubordination was endemic, so castles were razed and many a head fell. The crimes were duelling, an extravagant pastime which could account for 4,000 deaths in a single year, and rebellion, the chief protagonist of which was the King's brother, Gaston of Orleans, who encompassed the destruction of his fellow conspirators, and regularly saved himself, by a tedious routine of plot, betrayal, confession and pardon.

The course of the Thirty Years War (1618–1648) suggested the grave threat of a Hapsburg dominated Europe. France, having

Reverse of Richelieu medal, 1630
*(Bibliothèque Nationale, Paris. Cabinet des Médailles)*

profited by the brilliantly cynical diplomacy of Father Joseph, entered the struggle formally in 1635 for reasons of coldly calculated power politics. The skill with which these affairs were conducted led to the posthumous triumph of King and Cardinal at the Peace of Westphalia (1648), where foundations were firmly laid for the subsequent expansionist activities of Louis XIV.

The partnership of Louis and Richelieu was strong enough to survive the jealousy of nobles, Queen Mother and Queen. Centralized power was achieved by middle-class civil servants – the *Intendants*, dispatched throughout France; foreign affairs prospered – but the spirit and the mind also thrived. Religion was enlivened by the charm of Saint François de Sales and the charity of Saint Vincent de Paul; Madame de Rambouillet was the first to exercise the civilizing influence of the *salon*, Descartes had published his *Discours de la Méthode*, masterpieces by Corneille had been performed and the *Académie Française* founded before 1643 – by which year *Le Grand Siècle* had been firmly launched.

Louis XIV

*(Bibliothèque Nationale, Estampes, Paris)*

# LOUIS XIV, 1643-1715

## (Son of LOUIS XIII and Anne of Austria)

Born 1638, was 4 when he ascended the throne, and 76 when he died.

Married Maria Theresa, daughter of Philip IV of Spain, and had six children, one son, only, surviving infancy:

Louis the Dauphin

Both the Dauphin and *his* son Louis, Duke of Burgundy, predeceased Louis XIV.

*Thumbnail Sketch* Able, industrious, religious, amorous – and, beyond measure, proud – Louis XIV imposed his resplendent personality upon France and Europe. Never has there been so professional a monarch.

## WHAT TO KNOW

Louis XIII had appointed, by will, a council designed to restrict the powers of his widow as Regent. However, the Parliament of Paris, happy to stress its own constitutional importance, welcomed the *Lit de Justice* whereby the infant Louis XIV reversed this decision and gave Anne of Austria a free hand.

With the Italian Mazarin as her first minister (and perhaps, secretly, her husband – this cardinal had never been ordained priest) Anne prosecuted the war successfully until the Peace of Westphalia (1648) left a defeated Empire, a divided and exhausted Germany and a golden future for France. However, Mazarin's attempts to discipline the Parliament and his unpopularity with the nobles led to the *Fronde* rebellions of 1648–1652, in which Louis' tempestuous cousin *La Grande Mademoiselle* (daughter of Gaston of Orleans) maintained her family's tradition of insurrection. The outcome was a triumph for the Crown, and young Louis resolved to exercise absolutism from a centre other than his disrespectful capital, when the time should come. But France and Spain remained at war until the Peace of the Pyrenees (1659), as a result of which Louis married the Infanta Maria Theresa. Her unpaid dowry was later held to justify frequent claims to expansion at Spain's expense.

In 1661 Mazarin died and the twenty-two-year-old King took over personally. The brilliantly ambitious Superintendent of Finances, Fouquet, whose private accounts were inextricably and criminally mixed with those of France, and whose fêtes at Vaux-le-Vicomte aroused the jealous suspicion of his royal guest, was imprisoned for life. Finance, industry and commerce were now controlled by Colbert, an able, conscientious bourgeois (example of the diminished status of ministers), who followed the path of Henry IV and Sully, even to the extent of shirking that fundamental reform of the fiscal system, without which the eventual ruin of the monarchy was inevitable.

Colbert's efforts might have made France peacefully prosperous had it not been for his own tariffs, the King's passion for building and desire for territorial expansion, and the nation's bellicosity. With his army reformed by Louvois, his siege technique and fortifications perfected by Vauban, his navy expanded, Louis waged some thirty-one years of war between 1661 and 1714. To attack the Dutch (1672) was folly, even though this move had Colbert's strong support, for the implacable William of Orange could later direct England's power against France. To accept the will of Charles II of Spain (1700), whereby Louis' grandson, Philip of Anjou, inherited the Spanish throne, was wise, for such a treasure could not be relinquished to Austria. War-weary erstwhile enemies would probably have acquiesced, had not Louis perpetrated a number of inexplicably provocative acts (recognizing the Old Pretender as King of England was one) which precipitated the War of the Spanish Succession (1701–1714). Territorial expansion had been achieved (the extent of France, in 1714, was, with the exception of Lorraine, much as it is today), but at the cost of exhaustion and the rise of rival powers.

All activity sprang from Louis. Mistresses (Louise de la Vallière, Madame de Montespan and others) neither disturbed his 6–8 hours' daily business with the secretaries of state nor his religious observances, always punctilious, but genuinely

Boulle: Mazarine Chest of Drawers
*(Château of Versailles. Photo des Musées Nationaux)*

devout after his secret marriage with Madame de Maintenon
(governess to his children by the Montespan) on Maria Theresa's
death (1683). His most significant act of religious policy was the
Revocation of the Edict of Nantes (1685) which lost him, by
emigration, some 250,000 excellent Huguenot subjects. Louis
found his "métier du roi . . . grand, noble, délicieux"; he *ought* to
have said: "L'état c'est moi."

Memorial to all this is the Château of Versailles, less easy of
access now, through democratic guichets, than when "correct
dress" was the only requirement for admission to watch the *Grand
Monarque* eating his Gargantuan repasts or pacing Le Nôtre's
gardens. Policy, and a *tour de force* of personality, solved Louis'
overmighty subject problem by making it ridiculous for great
nobles to reside elsewhere. Saint-Simon pictures them, disciplined
by etiquette, emasculated by artificiality, but privileged to gaze
at Le Brun's ceilings, to laugh with Molière, weep with Racine
and tremble deliciously before Bossuet, imposing a cultural sway
over Europe in their stylized revolutions round *Le Roi Soleil*.

But "the last rays of the setting Sun King lit up great banks of
cloud. The Revolution was only the length of his own reign away".
(J. B. Firth.)

# CLASSICAL  Part 2
## 1715–1814

| | |
|---|---|
| Louis XV | 1715–1774 |
| Louis XVI  Part 1 | 1774–1789 |
| Part 2 | 1789–1792 |
| First Republic | 1792–1804 |
| The Convention | 1792–1795 |
| The Directory | 1795–1799 |
| The Consulate | 1799–1804 |
| Napoleon I | 1804–1814 |

*(In England cf. GEORGIAN 1702–1830)*

| | |
|---|---|
| George I | 1714–1727 |
| George II | 1727–1760 |
| George III | 1760–1820 |

CLASSICAL. Part II
The Petit Trianon, Versailles
(French Government Tourist Office)

# CLASSICAL Part 2
## 1715–1814

The cheerfully ebullient style known as *baroque*, which had its origin in the Italian Counter-Reformation, is, above all, associated with church interiors proffering a heavenly future which does not weigh too seriously upon the earthly present. Enormously successful in central Europe, it never drove French architects into uncontrolled bizarrerie. Its more restrained and elegant successor, *rococo* – seen at its best, perhaps, in Potsdam's Sans-Souci and Munich's Amalienburg – is often regarded by French critics as what one might call "Louis Quinze export". In this category may be placed de Corny's work at Nancy, started in 1752, for the Duchy of Lorraine (though long a sphere of French influence) did not revert finally to the French crown until the death of Stanislas Leczinski in 1766. Nonetheless the early years of Louis XV did witness a reaction against the ponderous classicism of the Grand Monarque, but there was a tightening of discipline again from the 1750s onwards, which produced such gems as J. A. Gabriel's Place Louis XV (later Place de la Révolution, now Place de la Concorde), palace of Compiègne and Petit Trianon. Thus the trend towards neo-classicism had, perhaps, already started when serious excavations began at Pompeii in 1755. The fact that these were pushed forward briskly under the direction of the French Empire, between 1806 and 1814, had the result of driving French architects into straight imitation – as exemplified by the Paris Madeleine. This famous and, indeed, handsome church, commissioned by Napoleon I as a tribute to his glorious armies (and the first to resound with the strains of Chopin's funeral march, at the obsequies of the composer in 1849), is about as original in conception as the Parthenon at Nashville, Tennessee.

Louis XV, by **Hyacinthe Rigaud** 1659–1743
*(Château of Versailles. Photo Giraudon)*

# LOUIS XV, 1715-1774

(Son of Louis, Duke of Burgundy, and Marie Adelaide of Savoy. Great-grandson of LOUIS XIV)

Born 1710, was 5 when he ascended the throne, and 64 when he died.

Married Maria Leczinska, daughter of Stanislas Leczinski, ex-King of Poland, and had one son:
    Louis the Dauphin, who predeceased him
and six daughters, including:
    Louise Elizabeth, who married Philip, Duke of Parma, son of Philip V of Spain

*Thumbnail Sketch* Undemonstrative in public, though not without charm, this idle monarch devoted the greater part of his time to extravagant pleasures, amongst which dalliance and the chase took priority.

## WHAT TO KNOW

Once again an infant inherited France and, by the now familiar *Lit de Justice* routine, gave a free hand to the Regent, Philip of Orleans, nephew to Louis XIV and a brilliant roué. Aristocratic councils replaced bourgeois ministers and foreign policy was reversed by a Triple Alliance with England and Holland (1717) followed by a short war with Spain. An original attempt was made to deal with the inherited debt, but the over-adventurous, if not necessarily dishonest, paper transactions of the Scottish banker John Law, which stimulated industry and commerce, led to a full-scale crash and the precipitate flight of the promoter.

Orleans died in 1723, the Duke of Bourbon (first minister) married Louis to Maria Leczinska, and in 1726 Louis' tutor, the seventy-three-year-old Cardinal Fleury, became first minister until his death aged ninety. Although Fleury's intentions were pacific, wars ensued. An attempt to reinstate Stanislas (War of the Polish Succession 1733-1735) was abortive, but, at the Peace of Vienna, this displaced potentate received the Duchy of Lorraine, which reverted to France on his death (1766). Again, in 1740, when the young Frederick the Great seized Silesia from the new Hapsburg Queen Maria Theresa, France, like Prussia, ignored the Pragmatic Sanction, which guaranteed Maria Theresa's inheritance, and joined in the War of the Austrian Succession. Several reverses had been suffered when Fleury died. The war, enlivened by the personal appearance of George II of England to defeat the French at Dettingen (1743), and by Louis XV's assistance at the avenging victory of Fontenoy (1745), closed with the fruitless peace of Aix-la-Chapelle (1748) and the restoration of the *status quo ante bellum*, while Louis recognized Frederick the Great's right to Silesia and that of the Hanoverians to the British crown.

In 1745 Louis had been captivated by Madame de Pompadour, a bourgeoise of beauty and intelligence, his mistress for five years and his friend until her death in 1764. During the uneasy peace (1748–1756) she was not without influence upon the European "diplomatic revolution" which allied Austria and France in one camp, and Prussia and England in the other. Frederick the Great, fearing for Silesia, opened the Seven Years War (1756–1763) by attacking Austria. England and France were soon at grips, with momentous results. France, defeated in Europe, defeated overseas, with Louisiana ceded to Spain, lost (except for a few factories) the India of Dupleix and the Canada of Montcalm. At the Peace of Paris she saw her Empire replaced by that of Britain.

Eleven years remained. The ageing satyr, after a period of

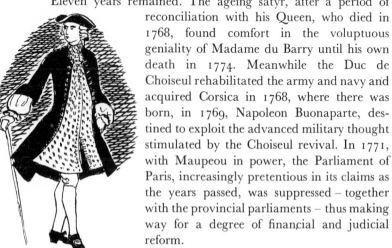

reconciliation with his Queen, who died in 1768, found comfort in the voluptuous geniality of Madame du Barry until his own death in 1774. Meanwhile the Duc de Choiseul rehabilitated the army and navy and acquired Corsica in 1768, where there was born, in 1769, Napoleon Buonaparte, destined to exploit the advanced military thought stimulated by the Choiseul revival. In 1771, with Maupeou in power, the Parliament of Paris, increasingly pretentious in its claims as the years passed, was suppressed – together with the provincial parliaments – thus making way for a degree of financial and judicial reform.

Recumbent Girl. (François Boucher 1751)
*(Wallraf-Richartz Museum, Cologne. Rheinisches Bildarchiv)*

The reign was inglorious, the period distinguished. The famous
Encyclopaedia was coming out between 1751 and 1772, the names
of Montesquieu, Rousseau, Diderot and – above all – Voltaire
were on the lips of aristocratic and bourgeois intellectuals, their
works in the hands of the enlightened despots. Salon walls glowed
with the canvases of Watteau, Boucher and Fragonard; Marivaux
enchanted and stimulated the playgoer. Scientific inquiry was
intense – Maupertuis measured meridians, Réaumur observed his
thermometer, soon Montgolfier's balloons would sway in the
heavens. Gastronomists throughout Europe rejoiced in French
cooking and French wines, while Frederick the Great, in Potsdam's
"Sans-Souci", observed that French was the language of the cultivated from Lisbon to Petersburg and from Stockholm to Naples.

Louis XVI. Copy of portrait by Duplessis 1725–1802
*(Musée Condé, Chantilly. Photo Giraudon)*

# LOUIS XVI, 1774–1792

(Son of Louis the Dauphin and Maria Josepha of Saxony, grandson of LOUIS XV)

## Part 1, 1774–1789

Born 1754, was 19 when he ascended the throne, 38 when the monarchy was abolished and when he was executed.

Married Marie Antoinette of Austria, and had four children, including:

> Marie Thérèse – married Louis, Duke of Angoulême
> Louis – died 1789
> LOUIS XVII (born 1785, died ? 1795)

*Thumbnail Sketch* Devout, courageous, no fool and a good locksmith. A great hunter and, despite excessive eating and drinking, an admirable family man. Indecisive and easily influenced, he was cursed with a lethargic insensitivity to what was really important.

## WHAT TO KNOW

The country which the new King inherited had witnessed a great population increase during the century and now counted some 26 million inhabitants – divided, as of old, into the three Estates of Clergy (130,000), Nobility (400,000) and the remainder, known as the Third Estate, of whom at least 20 million were peasants. The higher ranks in the Church were, by now, entirely recruited from the aristocracy, the nobility had been staging a come-back from the days when Louis XIV had enervated them into irresponsible impotence at Versailles – but both were divided by the jealousy of "have-nots" (village priests and country squireens) for "haves" (*haut clergé* and *haute noblesse*). The bourgeoisie, of steadily growing importance, consisted of many grades and engaged in foreign trade, internal commerce, industry, the professions and shopkeeping. There was also a proletariat, urban and rural, fulfilling the humbler tasks of city life and, in the case of the vast majority, tilling the soil, mainly for subsistence.

The century had, also, been one of ideas. The theories of the "Enlightenment", as expressed by philosophers in the Encyclopaedia and other works, had spread, as censorship relaxed, engendering a critical attitude towards contemporary institutions and, particularly, giving rise to anti-clericalism. But it would be unsound to regard these writers as a "think-tank" which produced that confused and essentially unplanned series of events which historians call "The French Revolution". Flirtation with new conceptions did not stop the First and Second Estates defending their privileges, did not convince the aristocracy of the virtues of the career open to talent, nor did it prevent their increasing strictness in the exaction of feudal dues – but it did send volunteers across the Atlantic, notably La Fayette, from 1776 onwards, to fight for American independence. These men were to bring back the ideal of liberty, war was to precipitate a financial crisis, and the bourgeoisie, frustrated politically and socially, were to find themselves leading a revolution "out to the undiscovered ends", of which none had dreamed in the 1770s and 1780s.

There had been expansion both of commerce and industry in eighteenth-century France, with wealth accruing to these same bourgeois, increasingly irritated that other avenues of promotion were blocked to them, and even the lot of the peasants was happier than that of their counterparts in other European countries. But prices were rising and small men, whose wages did not increase proportionately, suffered. The 1780s saw a decreased productivity

– tending towards a slump – and official French participation in the American War of Independence (an alliance was signed with the United States in 1778) brought the government to the verge of bankruptcy.

What, in fact, had government action been? Louis XVI, warmly welcomed on his accession, had restored the Parliaments – suppressed by his predecessor – and had appointed Turgot as Controller of Finances. Turgot, amongst other reforms, essayed the expedient of a general land tax, but the Parliaments were swiftly up in arms in defence of privilege, for French fiscal affairs were bedevilled by reason of the fact that the Nobility were vir-

Mantel Clock. The case attributed to
Pierre Philippe Thomire (1751–1843)
*( Reproduced by permission of the Trustees of the Wallace Collection)*

tually exempt from direct taxation, while the Clergy were only
under obligation to produce a "Free Gift", which they voted on
terms not unfavourable to themselves. So Turgot went and the
project was temporarily dropped. Necker, the Swiss banker, took
over from 1776 to 1781, borrowed hugely and produced a *tour
de force* budget statement showing a comfortable surplus when,
in fact, the deficit was enormous. In 1783 the brilliant Calonne did
much to restore confidence, but, after three years, appreciated the
full gravity of the situation and returned to the idea of the Land
Tax. 1786 also saw an unfavourable commercial treaty with
England, which caused widespread unemployment. An Assembly
of Notables, hand-picked by the King, turned down Calonne's
suggestions in 1787, and their repetition received similar treatment
when put to the Parliament of Paris by Calonne's successor,
Loménie de Brienne (a favourite of Louis' Queen Marie
Antoinette – whose unfortunately frivolous behaviour, culminating in the notorious Diamond Necklace Affair of 1785, did so much
to bring the monarchy into disrepute). The Royal authority had, in
fact, been flouted by the privileged classes. It was, thus, *they* who
started the French Revolution, and in the year 1787. This is what
is known as "the aristocratic revolt", and it led to the calling of the
Estates General in 1789, the first time since 1614!

# LOUIS XVI, 1774–1792

## Part 2, 1789–1792

**WHAT TO KNOW** *(continued)*

Chance operated during the years 1788–1789. The 1788 harvest was bad, the winter severe. The Estates General were summoned to Versailles, a location dangerously near the volatile and hungry capital, but the King would have his hunting. And if one factor is to be selected as the motive force which kept the wheels of revolution turning during the next few years, it is grain scarcity and expensive bread.

And so there assembled some 300 clergy, 290 nobles and 600 of the Third Estate. The latter, persuaded by Siéyès that they were "the Nation", naturally wished that the 1,190-odd should meet, discuss and vote together – for thus, with their sympathizers amongst the clerics and aristocrats, they would command the majority to which they felt entitled. At the opening session, however (5 May 1789), after enduring a 180-minute speech from Necker, the orders were asked to withdraw and decide separately the subjects which they were prepared to treat in common. Such a procedure, and a single vote per order, would frequently put the Third Estate in a minority of 1 to 2, so they opposed it stubbornly and, on 17 June 1789, proclaimed themselves "The National Assembly".

It was now decided to hold a Royal Session and on 20 June, as a result of administrative incompetence, the Third Estate were locked out of their meeting place. Fearing coercion, they jostled into a nearby tennis court and swore to remain together until France had a constitution. Three days later the Royal Session quashed their pronouncements, outlined reforms, but made clear that there would be no forcible curtailment of clerical and noble privilege. At its close the Third Estate ignored the King's order to disperse, remained seated, with Mirabeau thundering that bayonets alone would remove them, while Louis shrugged his shoulders and let them be. On 24 and 25 June they were joined by liberal priests and nobles – a trend sanctioned by Louis on 27 June when, perhaps panicking at rumours of brigands near Versailles, he ordered all the deputies to join up together. Thus, on 9 July 1789, the National Constituent Assembly found itself in being.

But the year was not to proceed quietly. Paris, where bread and work were both scarce, observed uneasily the concentration of Royal troops (Swiss and German) about Versailles. News of Necker's dismissal aroused indignation, and men feared for the Assembly. In the Palais Royal (property of Louis' cousin, the Duke of Orleans, a family traditionally hostile to the Kings of France) agitators incited the citizens to arms. A body of 407, the Electors of the Paris Third Estate deputies, formed a municipal government and attempted to take command. Crowds surged to and fro and, on 14 July, one of them, numbering some 800 minor tradesmen and artisans, in search of muskets and powder, advanced upon the Bastille. The muddled operation resulting in the fall of this fortress has become one of the great symbolic acts of history. The Electors now took over Paris, Necker was recalled, a National Guard, sporting the new tricolour, was formed under La Fayette, the King, wearing its cockade, appeared in his capital, which had, in fact, assured the continuation of the Revolution. As the summer went on a number of important provincial cities staged similar risings, while the countryside was swept by disturbances directed against feudal privilege and landlords' rights, accompanied by a curious malaise known as "The Great Fear". The Assembly reacted dramatically. On the night of 4 August feudalism was voted away and, on the 26th, there appeared "The Declaration of the Rights of Man and of the Citizen". Autumn brought bread riots and Parisians were alarmed at the arrival of the Flanders regiment in Versailles. Disquieting reports of reactionary behaviour at a guest night spread abroad, and, as October opened, men were saying that the King ought to reside in Paris. And so, on 5 October, came the march of the women (followed by La Fayette with 20,000 National Guardsmen) to Versailles and the return with them, next day, of the Royal family – "the baker, the baker's wife and the baker's son". The Assembly followed, and a portentous year ended with an attempt to stave off bankruptcy by the nationalization of Church property and the issue of the paper money known as *"assignats"*.

1790 passed restlessly. Many nobles emigrated, while the Royal

Family settled down to a restricted life in the Tuileries. There were breaches of service discipline and reports of corn convoys tempting the hungry to acts of violence. The Assembly optimistically renounced war, nobility was abolished and, on 12 July, there was voted "The Civil Constitution of the Clergy". This was the logical sequel to the nationalization of Church property, which had made the state responsible for ecclesiastical financial arrangements. It provided sensible geographical changes in dioceses and parishes, to fit in with the new division of France into departments, and a much-needed readjustment of stipends. But it also laid down the local election of priests and bishops, who would henceforth submit, in matters of discipline, to the state – and all this without reference to the Pope. The Church was now a branch of the Civil Service and the idea of the Divine Society abandoned. An oath accepting these rulings was required of all ecclesiastics – and refused by the vast majority of bishops, most of whom left the country. The priests were split, approximately half and half, into those who became "constitutional" and those who remained "refractory" – a position which hardened when Pius VI condemned the proceedings in April 1791.

This same month saw the death of the great Mirabeau – whose advice had been available to the King and Queen, even if his character aroused their mistrust. Disquieted by Royal impo-

tence in Paris, Mirabeau had counselled withdrawal from the capital (as long as it did not entail moving to a frontier) followed by an appeal to the nation. Distressed in conscience by the new ecclesiastical arrangements, Louis now put into operation the disastrous idea of moving secretly to an armed camp at Montmédy, 172 miles to the North East. Meticulously planned by a young Swedish nobleman called Fersen, reputedly Marie Antoinette's lover, it came to grief with the arrest of the escapers at Varennes (21 June 1791) – due to a mixture of Royal lethargy, military incompetence and popular initiative. Back came the fugitives to a sullen Paris, the King underwent suspension and was reinstated after about three weeks, but an anti-monarchical demonstration suffered the so-called "Massacre of the Champ de Mars" of 17 July, and the Republican movement was born. Nevertheless the King's acceptance of a new constitution, not unlike that of Great Britain, gave rise to guarded optimism when the National Constituent Assembly was dissolved and the new Legislative Assembly met on 1 October 1791.

The new body, from which members of the old were excluded, was dominated by a group called the Girondins, because many of their leaders came from the Bordeaux area. These amateur, provincial politicians, fearing the émigrés and the old powers of Europe, also believed in the cleansing properties of war. King and court supported them, seeing the possibility of a comeback in time of crisis. They were opposed by the Jacobins – political professionals, metropolitan, often republicans, and realizing fully the dangers of the hostilities which they were later to prosecute with such vigour. War was declared on Austria on 20 April 1792 – thus bringing the Emperor Francis II, and Prussia, into the field against France. The enemy, preoccupied with Russia's designs on Poland, acted slowly, but, even so, a French offensive in Belgium ended in disaster. Louis quarrelled with, and dismissed, his Girondin ministers, and, on 20 June, a mob invaded the Tuileries. From this point onwards anti-monarchism grew apace, exacerbated at the end of July when a manifesto issued by the Duke of Brunswick, commanding the Austro-Prussian forces, reached Paris. This inept document threatened all Frenchmen who opposed the Royal authority and lit the train leading to the explosion of 10 August 1792, when the Tuileries were again invaded, the Swiss Guards massacred, and the Royal family – forced to throw themselves upon the mercy of the Assembly – retained in custody. The King was now suspended, La Fayette deserted, and, as August turned into September, Brunswick advanced through Longwy and Verdun. Paris, fearing a fifth column in its teeming prisons, perpetrated the September massacres. But, on 20 September, the cannonade of Valmy halted the enemy, Goethe declared: "From this day and this hour dates a new epoch in world history", and on 21 September the Convention replaced the Legislative Assembly. On that same day the monarchy was abolished.

Robespierre

Danton

Marat

Camille Desmoulins

Philippe Égalité

Carnot

Fouquier Tinville

*(Bibliothèque Nationale, Estampes, Paris)*

# THE FIRST REPUBLIC
## The Convention, 1792–1795

## WHAT TO KNOW

In the developments just recounted the city of Paris, as represented by its municipal body – the Commune – had played a major part. It enjoyed the support of the Jacobin, leftist members of the new Convention – men like Robespierre, Danton, Marat, Camille Desmoulins and the Duke of Orleans (now transmogrified into "Philippe Egalité"). Sitting on the higher benches of the Convention's meeting place these, and their adherents, were known as "The Mountain". They were opposed by the more numerous Girondins, and the two groups did battle for the allegiance of the "Plain" – as the mass of centre deputies was called. In this the Girondins were ineffective. They opposed the Commune and so, in their provincial way, offended Paris. They attacked Danton and Robespierre – dangerous enemies, too formidable for them. They incurred suspicion by trying to save the King from the guillotine – first established in the capital (August 1792) on the Place du Carrousel, and subsequently moved to the Place de la Révolution (modern Place de la Concorde). Here, on 21 January 1793, Louis met his death, by now a "cruel necessity", with dignity and fortitude.

With this event the war clouds thickened. Early in 1793 Austria, Prussia, England, Holland and Spain – fearing the new virus of Liberty, Equality and Fraternity – formed the First Coalition against France. General Dumouriez, recently minister of war, but now commanding in the Netherlands, suffered defeat at Neerwinden (18 March) and deserted. To face the crisis was formed the Committee of Public Safety – twelve able, industrious, ruthless men, constituting what was, virtually, a War Cabinet. And crisis it was. Provincial revolts against the power of Paris were encouraged by the Girondins. In the capital the Commune moved again and once more the Tuileries, where the Convention sat, saw armed violence, leading to the purge of the Girondins on 2 June. In July one of their young, female sympathizers – Charlotte Corday – murdered Marat, and the Terror, which had started six weeks previously, was really on. Never had France experienced such rigid centralization. The *enquêteurs* of St. Louis and Richelieu's *intendants* were nothing to the "Representatives on Mission" who toured the country for the Committee of Public Safety. Prices and wages were strictly controlled, hoarders and black marketeers were punished, the Committee of General Security (handling police affairs) rounded up suspects – whom the Revolutionary Tribunal, dominated by the tireless Public Prosecutor, Fouquier-Tinville, tried with dispatch. In Paris more than 2,000 victims, of all classes, were decapitated, including, as autumn came, Marie Antoinette (16 October 1793). Other parts of France saw variations on this theme, of which Fouché's shootings at Lyons and Carrier's drownings at Nantes are notorious. With all this, Christianity was officially replaced by the worship of Reason, and a new Revolutionary Calendar, inspired by the poetry of agriculture and seasonal change, faced Frenchmen with unfamiliar months (*Frimaire*, *Floréal*, etc.), while Saints' Days gave way to homely festivals in honour of the pumpkin, the turnip, the pig, the barrel and the dungheap. All this was, in fact, part of a major war effort. Carnot created, for the first time in modern history, a nation in arms. Victorious generals were loaded with honours, the unsuccessful were punished with death. The reverses of 1793 turned into the glories of 1794, when young commanders

began to practise the doctrines of French eighteenth-century military thinkers and technicians, whilst all ranks demonstrated the truth of Napoleon's maxim: "In war, moral considerations make up three-quarters of the game."

Politics remained dangerous. A democratically minded group led by the journalist Hébert attempted a revolt against the committee, and heads fell. Then the rivalry between Jacobin and Girondin was replaced by that between Danton and Robespierre. Danton – the warm, coarse, untidy advocate, whose thundering eloquence captivated the working-class of the Cordeliers district of Paris – stood so high after 10 August 1792 that he was "the voice of the Revolution and of France"

The Fountain of Regeneration, 10 August 1793
*(Bibliothèque Nationale, Estampes, Paris)*

(Michelet). He was ousted from the Committee of Public Safety when the coldly fastidious Robespierre joined it in July 1793, and gradually became associated with those who wished to abate the Terror, which was the main reason for his rivals bringing him to execution in April 1794. For Robespierre believed in virtue and "severe, inflexible justice". He also believed in the immortality of the soul, and virtually set himself up as the High Priest of the Cult of the Supreme Being – established in 1794. The revolt of the ordinary man against puritan standards, the tightened belt and the busy scaffold (as the war news improved), together with fear, and discord on the overworked Committee, eventually led to the arrest of the Robespierreists and their execution on 28 July 1794 (10 Thermidor, Year II).

There was now a period of sharp reaction, the teeth of the committee were drawn, the Commune went and, after a year, a new constitution was produced. This provoked a rising in Paris, which was suppressed on 13 Vendémiaire (5 October) by a young artillery general called Buonaparte. The National Convention was superseded by the Directory.

Paul Barras – a Director throughout
*(Bibliothèque Nationale, Estampes, Paris)*

# THE FIRST REPUBLIC
## The Directory, 1795–1799

### WHAT TO KNOW

The new constitution provided two assemblies – a lower house (Council of Five Hundred, minimum age 30) and an upper house (Council of Ancients, married or widowers, minimum age 40). These were persons of substance, elected by persons of substance (there were five million voters). Two-thirds of the deputies had been members of the Convention, one-third of them were now to retire annually. Above, as executive, stood the Directory – a quintet from which one member withdrew each year, as determined by lot.

The press accorded to this administration has been, until lately, inadequate or bad. It should be remembered that its stringent financial measures (e.g. the repudiation of two-thirds of the national debt in 1797) were an effort to cope with inherited crises, and that its policy in direct taxation was followed for almost 120 years. Even its *coups d'état*, now against left, now against right, were, arguably, an exhibition of political skill. Its eventual adoption of dictatorial methods was certainly an attempt to remedy inherent instability, and to protect republicanism from a royalist restoration.

By November 1795, when the Directory assumed power, the external enemies of France were fewer, for, between April and July, the First Coalition had been depleted by treaties of peace made between the Republic and Prussia, Holland and Spain. Thus tension continued to relax and, at home, the reaction against austerity gathered momentum. There was pleasure for those who could afford it – though the less well-off faced bread prices which, in 1795, stood at double those of 1789. Extravagant *incroyables* led scantily dressed *merveilleuses* into dance halls and theatres. Gambling and gastronomy flourished. In opulent *salons* men admired the creole charms of Josephine de Beauharnais (bride of young General Bonaparte on 9 March 1796), the wit and *embonpoint* of Madame de Staël (Necker's daughter), the much-imitated fashions of Madame Tallien, and the breathtaking beauty of eighteen-year-old Madame Récamier.

Pleasure, for some, there might be. Peace there was not. Britain would not permit serious competition for world markets by her bellicose hereditary foe, and viewed France's occupation of Belgium with traditional distaste. Austria remained an implacable ideological enemy and feared the revival of those ambitions which, over the centuries, had sent French armies to Italy.

Indeed Italy with its wealth – agricultural, urban and artistic – tempted the impoverished Directory. Here, too, a blow at the Austrian overlord would assist the advance on Vienna, by the Black Forest–Danube route, planned for Generals Moreau and Jourdan. The Italian operation was entrusted to twenty-six-year-old General Bonaparte, who, by a year's brilliant campaign in the modern manner (1796–1797), bustled the enemy from Lombardy and negotiated the Peace of Campo Formio, whereby France officially acquired Belgium, the Rhine provinces and the Ionian Islands, the Cisalpine Republic came into being in Northern Italy and the Republic of Venice was sacrificed, as compensation, to the defeated power.

The problem of Britain remained. It was appreciated that she could best be hit in Egypt, whither Bonaparte sailed, surrounded by soldiers, technicians and scholars, in May 1798. He was to "drive the English from all their positions in the East which he could reach". Avoiding Nelson, he captured Malta from the Knights of St. John and reached Egypt on 1 July. "Forty centuries now looked down" upon the battle of the Pyramids, Nelson's destruction of the French fleet at the Nile, the invasion of Syria, the deciphering of the Rosetta stone hieroglyphics and, on receipt of news from Europe that the French had lost Italy and been defeated on the Rhine, the hand-over of command to Kléber and Bonaparte's departure for France in a fast frigate.

Here was crisis. Alarmed by the advance of French arms and ideas, a Second Coalition (England, Russia, Austria, Turkey, the Neapolitan Bourbons and Portugal) had been formed. The Directory was hard pressed. Domestic exigencies had already induced violations of the Constitution and advocates of a stronger executive were not lacking. Siéyès had a plan which, for its fulfilment, required a soldier. The soldier was now to hand. After some weeks of planning, on 9 November 1799 (18 Brumaire), the

General Augereau at the bridge of Arcola. (Charles Thévenin)
*(Château of Versailles. Photo des Musées Nationaux)*

Councils were moved to St. Cloud, on grounds of an alleged leftist conspiracy in Paris. Next day, amidst scenes of extraordinary muddle and ineptitude (during which Lucien Bonaparte, President of the Council of Five Hundred, saved the situation for his brother), the Directory was dissolved and three Consuls (Bonaparte, Roger-Ducos and Siéyès) were nominated to rule France and produce yet another new constitution.

Bonaparte as First Consul by J. R. Smith – after Appiani

*(Bibliothèque Nationale, Estampes, Paris)*

# THE FIRST REPUBLIC
## The Consulate, 1799–1804

## WHAT TO KNOW

On 15 December 1799 France was presented with the Constitution of the year VIII and, after times of uncertainty and trial, placed her confidence, demonstrated by a plebiscite, in an authoritarian régime. The First of the three Consuls, and principal architect of the new régime, Bonaparte, enjoyed formidable powers. In his hands lay the decisions of war and peace, the promulgation of laws, the appointment of ministers, ambassadors and senior civil servants. He and his two colleagues, whose role was advisory, were to hold office for ten years. A Council of State, composed of his own extremely able nominees (Bonaparte believed in "the career open to talents") assisted him in concerting government measures. Three assemblies were normally happy to speed legislation on its way – the Tribunate discussing the Council's proposals, the Legislative Body listening in silence while Tribunes and Councillors put "pros" and "cons" before it – prior to recording its "yea" or "nay" by secret ballot. Finally the Senate was charged with the duty of ensuring the maintenance of the Constitution.

Bonaparte planned a rationalization and consolidation of French institutions, but it was hard to accomplish this task while the war continued unsuccessfully. In May 1800 he marched over the Alps by the reputedly impracticable Great St. Bernard Pass, to defeat the Austrians at Marengo. In December Moreau was victorious at Hohenlinden, 200 miles west of Vienna. Thus was Austria brought to sign the Peace of Lunéville (1801), which confirmed Campo Formio, leaving France established in Belgium and on the Rhine, with an ideological and political grip on satellite republics in Holland, Switzerland and Northern Italy. Even England yielded to war weariness in 1802, and accepted the Peace of Amiens with extravagant jubilation. But when the expected milk and honey failed to flow, when the islanders found France as hostile as ever to their commercial aspirations, as active as ever in military and naval preparations, and as blatant as ever in what seemed to them pure expansionist ambition – they refused to honour their treaty obligation to evacuate Malta, and the Peace (which all concerned really knew to be only a truce) came to an end in May 1803. But if military success is often transitory, many of the remarkable civil achievements of the Consulate have lasted.

Bonaparte desired unity and, seeing in religion "not the mystery of the Incarnation, but the mystery of the social order", healed the schism caused by the Civil Constitution of the Clergy. By his Concordat of 1801 with Pius VII Catholicism was rightly seen (in a framework of general toleration) as the faith of the majority of Frenchmen, and was thus to be state-financed. Church appointments were a Government matter, canonical investiture that of the Pope. Pious souls were comforted and the "throne and altar" plank removed from the royalist platform. The Revolution had also left many lay institutions fluid – they were now tidied up by the greatest centralizer in French history. Prefects of departments, Sub-Prefects of *arrondissements* and Mayors of *communes* formed a chain of command, originating with the First Consul, which has stood the test of changing times, while the rolling drums of the Lycées summoned the young to good citizenship. Taxes were efficiently assessed and collected and the Bank of France founded. And there were rewards. "Men are led by toys," said Bonaparte, and gave his compatriots the Legion of Honour, with which they have played happily ever since. The judicial system created by the Constituent Assembly was maintained, while work on the codes (civil, civil procedure, criminal, penal and commercial) was, except in the case of the fourth, initiated now. In 1807 the first was entitled "Code Napoléon" and at St. Helena the exile observed: "My true glory consisted in the Civil Code."

Different glory was imminent. With the resumption of war Bonaparte established the Boulogne camp, for the invasion of England, and marched on Hanover. But treason was discovered in which Generals Pichegru and Moreau, with the Royalist insurgent Cadoudal, were involved. Pichegru committed suicide in prison, Moreau withdrew abroad and Cadoudal was executed. Meanwhile, to "encourage" the other Royalists, and bind French regicides to himself by joining them, Bonaparte, as a calculated act of policy, abducted the Duke of Enghien, scion of the House of

The French Army descends the St. Bernard. (A. Taunay)
*(Château of Versailles. Photo des Musées Nationaux)*

Condé, from Baden and had him summarily shot at Vincennes.
This shattering event had the effect which Bonaparte, no doubt,
foresaw. Royalist plots ceased and men began to favour the re-
establishment of hereditary government. The principle: "the
King is dead, long live the King" means that you cannot kill a
dynasty with one pistol shot. And the same applies to Emperors.
On 18 May 1804 the Senate declared Napoleon Bonaparte, who
had become First Consul for life in 1802, Emperor of the French.

Napoleon in his Study by Jacques-Louis David 1748–1825
(*National Gallery of Art, Washington D.C. Samuel H. Kress Collection*)

# NAPOLEON I, 1804–1814

(Son of Charles Marie de Buonaparte and his wife Letitia)

Born 1769, was 34 when proclaimed Emperor, 44 when he abdicated, and 51 when he died.

Married Josephine de Beauharnais, whom he divorced. No issue.
Married Marie Louise of Austria by whom he had one son:
> Napoleon Francis Joseph Charles, King of Rome, "Napoleon II", Duke of Reichstadt. Died 1832.

*Thumbnail Sketch*   Neither the best, nor yet the most pleasant, but possibly the greatest human being whom History records.

## WHAT TO KNOW

Napoleon's Empire, really the Consulate writ large, could, by its nature, never be at peace. War demands a firm hand, and this France experienced. Intellectual activity (except in science) was curtailed by censorship, nor, despite the merits of Gérard, David and Ingres, was there much art of great distinction. But a sense of command is not altogether distasteful to Frenchmen, who now benefited from efficient finance and enlightened public works which, together with industrial and agricultural progress, led to a temporarily improved standard of living.

The hostilities which opened in 1792 and ended in 1815 constitute one great struggle. French armies fought from Acre in the East to Vimeiro in the West and Moscow in the North, while Paris sights and streets acquired names like trumpets "silver pealing": Arcola, Rivoli, Pyramids, Aboukir, Marengo, Austerlitz, Jena, Friedland and Wagram. During this time anti-French coalitions formed and dissolved with a number of countries claiming the lion's share in Napoleon's overthrow: Spain, Austria, Russia, Prussia and England. The relentless hostility of the last-named is the clue to the whole matter. Its causes were fear of colonial and commercial competition and expansion in Europe and overseas. In 1793 Danton had defined the "natural frontiers of France" – North Sea, Rhine, Alps and Pyrenees – which places Belgium in French hands. The government of George III was neither the first nor the last to find intolerable the domination of that area by a hostile power, and Napoleon himself saw Antwerp as "a loaded pistol held at the head of England".

From Trafalgar onwards (21 October 1805) England's rule of the waves was absolute; similarly, after 2 December 1805 (Austerlitz) it was possible for Napoleon to dominate Europe. And such domination was necessary for the efficacy of the Continental System, announced by the Berlin Decree of November 1806, which forbad all commerce with Britain. So the long coastlines demanded a vast Empire, a series of satellite states and a number of allies. The peak was reached in 1810 when the Empire's eastern frontier ran from Lübeck on the Baltic, up the Rhine to Basle, and, skirting the enclave formed by the subservient Helvetic Confederation, swept on to include Piedmont, Genoa and Western Italy as far South as Gaeta with, beyond the Adriatic, the Illyrian provinces and Dalmatia. Under Napoleonic protection lay the Confederation of the Rhine, the Kingdoms of Italy and Naples and the Grand Duchy of Warsaw. To assist this enterprise members of the Bonaparte family were scattered about Europe in high places, providing three Kings, a Queen and a Grand Duchess. At the same time Prussia, the Austrian Empire (the Holy Roman Empire ended in 1806) and Russia were, allegedly, France's friends. Here, then, was a new "Ascendancy of France" under which many European countries felt the stimulus of scientific advance, career opportunity and administrative efficiency. The political futures of Italy and Germany were profoundly influenced. But despite Napoleon's efforts to render his Empire respectable – did not Pius VII attend his coronation? Had he not divorced Josephine? Could one fly higher than marriage with a Hapsburg Princess? Was there not a male heir? – the great structure remained brittle. Spanish nationalism awoke echoes elsewhere, eventually the Russian alliance could no longer be maintained and the march on Moscow ensued. In 1812 the remains of the Grand Army reeled back and the nations closed the ring at Leipzig (1813). The Emperor then fought a brilliant withdrawal action into an exhausted France, which led

Carriage of Empress Josephine
*(Mansell Collection)*

him to abdication, the "adieux" of Fontainebleau and, for a spell, to Elba. Meanwhile the late Imperial Councillor Talleyrand, now convinced of the desirability of a Bourbon restoration, welcomed the Tsar Alexander I to his Paris hotel.

# NINETEENTH CENTURY

## 1814–1914

| | |
|---|---|
| Louis XVIII | 1814–1824 |
| Charles X | 1824–1830 |
| Louis Philippe | 1830–1848 |
| Second Republic | 1848–1852 |
| Napoleon III | 1852–1870 |
| Third Republic | 1870–1940 |
|     Part 1   1870–1914 | |

*(In England cf. GEORGIAN 1702–1830;*
*VICTORIAN 1830–1901)*

| | |
|---|---|
| George III | 1760–1820 |
| George IV | 1820–1830 |
| William IV | 1830–1837 |
| Victoria | 1837–1901 |
| Edward VII | 1901–1910 |
| George V | 1910–1936 |

NINETEENTH CENTURY
The Opera, Paris

*(French Government Tourist Office)*

This building was greatly admired by Adolf Hitler
during his visit to Paris on 28 June 1940

# NINETEENTH CENTURY
## 1814–1914

It is hardly possible to make a tidy statement about nineteenth-century architecture – though it is true to say that the period saw a breakaway from the shackles of neo-classicism, of which the last monument is the Arc de Triomphe, started in 1806 and completed thirty years later. There was great development of materials: iron, cast-iron, cement, concrete and reinforced concrete – all these were exploited in revival, restoration and contemporary work. For there was revival of almost every building style known to history – and with it went restoration (N.B. the cast-iron spire of Rouen cathedral), stimulated by the pens of Montalembert and Victor Hugo, and associated, above all, with the name of Viollet-le-Duc, whose controversial work may be studied in place after place, from Amiens in the North to Carcassonne in the South and Vézelay in the East. On the contemporary level the astonishing mélange of the Paris Opera House (widely acclaimed at the time as the finest theatre in the world) stands as a memorial to the opulent society of the 1860s and 1870s – all part of the prosperity and progress celebrated by the exhibitions of 1855, 1867 and 1889. These have their monument in Gustave Eiffel's 980-foot tower (1887–1889), while the central markets of Paris (les Halles), with their roofs of iron and glass, are amongst the many examples of the transformation scene worked in his capital by the Emperor Napoleon III. In addition, between 1823 and 1891, over twenty thousand miles of railway line had been constructed – keeping architects busy on bridges and stations. In the course of one hundred years a world of new techniques had been revealed.

Louis XVIII, when Count of Provence, by Duplessis 1725–1802
(*Musée Condé, Chantilly. Photo Giraudon*)

# LOUIS XVIII, 1814–1824

(Son of Louis the Dauphin and Maria Josepha of Saxony, grandson of LOUIS XV and brother of LOUIS XVI whose son, LOUIS XVII, is presumed to have died in the Temple prison in 1795)

Born 1755, was 58 at the time of the first Restoration, and 68 when he died.

Married Louise Marie Josephine of Savoy. Was a childless widower in 1814.

*Thumbnail Sketch*  Though his ideas were those of the eighteenth century, this intelligent and humorous old gentleman understood the practical in politics, even if he lacked dynamism and glamour.

## WHAT TO KNOW

War-weary France was not ill-pleased to accept a Bourbon restoration. Louis XVIII regained his native land on 24 April 1814, promulgated a charter which referred unrealistically and tactlessly to "the nineteenth year of our reign", but guaranteed the liberties won during the Revolution and set up constitutional government with a two-Chamber legislature based on a franchise which was to remain limited until the declaration of universal suffrage in 1848. The King's intentions were, no doubt, impeccable, but his reactionary brother, the Count of Artois, and many members of the emigré entourage, alarmed those who had benefited from the Revolution and Empire. Peasants feared for their land, unemployed Napoleonic veterans suffered deep discontent. So "the Imperial Corsican" slipped away from Elba and embarked upon a gamble which swept him back to the Tuileries in triumph (20 March 1815), while Royalty was bustled off to Ghent.

Napoleon now presented to the French people, and to Europe, the picture of a liberal Empire, which by no means impressed his enemies gathered at the Congress of Vienna, who left his diplomatic communications unanswered and mobilized grimly. War was inevitable, and Napoleon decided to attack the allied forces in Belgium. His opening moves – swift concentration about Charleroi and onward advance towards Brussels – were masterly, and "humbugged" Wellington. But 18 June brought Waterloo and defeat at the hands of the Duke and Blücher, "a damned serious business . . . the nearest run thing you ever saw in your life", but prelude to the second abdication and the Imperial sunset over St. Helena. So ended the episode known to history as the "Hundred Days".

Back came Louis XVIII once again; a formidable allied army of occupation took up its positions; the frontiers of 1792, granted to France by the First Peace of Paris (1814), were reduced, by the cession of important strong points, to those of 1789; the Chamber of Deputies was thronged with Ultra-Royalists; Talleyrand and Fouché – Louis' first choice as ministers – had to go, and were succeeded by the Duke of Richelieu.

Richelieu, a man of integrity and sense, the friend of Czar Alexander I, and courageous governor of plague-striken Odessa when in exile, could not prevent something in the nature of a White Terror. The gallant Marshal Ney and the young Colonel Labédoyère, whose troops had welcomed the returning Napoleon at Grenoble, were shot. But this reactionary Chamber did not last long and was replaced, in 1816, by one more moderate in tone. Constructive financial measures facilitated swift payment of the war indemnity and, in November 1818, France was free of foreign troops.

But a liberal swing, gathering momentum, led to the King's selection of Count Decazes as first minister in December, and it was hoped that France, painfully split by the turmoil of thirty years, might become one in the pursuit of a middle way. However in 1820, year of the Cato Street Conspiracy, of the suppression of liberalism in Vienna, of revolts in Spain, Portugal, Naples and Mexico, a demented saddler named Louvel struck down the Duke of Berry, second son of the Count of Artois, as he left the Opera. Decazes fell, Richelieu returned on a wave of reaction, but soon gave way to Villèle, who was to remain in power until 1828. Royalist and right wing enthusiasm was increased by the birth of

Bureau Candelabra with cipher of Louis XVIII
*(Louvre, Paris. Photo des Musées Nationaux)*

a posthumous child to Berry, "l'enfant du miracle" and potential heir to France, for Louis XVIII and Artois' elder son, the Duke of Angoulême, were both childless.

On 5 May 1821, four thousand miles away, the great Napoleon died, while the French government, ironically enough, was seeking the glamour of successful war. This, sponsored by the illiberal rulers of Russia, Prussia and Austria, took place in Spain in 1823, whither Angoulême led an army which restored the despotic Ferdinand VII and encouraged royalist hearts to beat high. Thus it was that fear of a reactionary future haunted the deathbed of Louis XVIII (September 1824), who exhorted his successor, Artois, to exercise circumspection, above all in the honouring of the Charter.

Charles X, when Count of Artois, by Danloux 1745–1806

*( Musée Condé, Chantilly. Photo Giraudon)*

# CHARLES X, 1824–1830

(Son of Louis the Dauphin and Maria Josepha of Saxony.
Brother of LOUIS XVIII)

Born 1757, was 66 when he ascended the throne, and 72 when he abdicated.

Married Maria Theresa of Sardinia and had two sons:
> Louis, Duke of Angoulême, who married Marie Thérèse, daughter of Louis XVI
> Charles, Duke of Berry, who married Caroline of Naples

*Thumbnail Sketch*  Profligate in ˙youth, devout in maturity, this charming but anachronistic protagonist of the *Ancien Régime* really *had* "learnt nothing and forgotten nothing".

## WHAT TO KNOW

Queen Victoria's favourite uncle – Leopold, King of the Belgians – may have been right in thinking Charles X a more agreeable person than Louis XVIII. He was certainly a worse monarch.

More robust than his predecessor, he relished the fatiguing and provocative pomp of a traditional coronation at Rheims, while financial compensation for emigrés, followed by a law which made sacrilege a capital offence, alarmed those Frenchmen who dreaded reaction, undue papal influence and Jesuitry. Villèle battled on as chief minister, the liberal Casimir Périer offered determined opposition, Béranger wrote Bonapartist songs, Paris murmured, and the National Guard positively shouted its support for the Charter, when reviewed by Charles in 1827. It was disbanded immediately and a press censorship clamped down. The unfavourable results of elections in November that year led to Villèle's resignation in January 1828.

There followed rather more than twelve months during which Charles entrusted the government to an able politician, de Martignac, who eventually fell before the combined fire of Right and Left, a fate frequently suffered by men of the Centre.

Charles now turned with relief to Prince Jules de Polignac, whose mother had been a close friend of Marie Antoinette and

whose *Ancien Régime* opinions were dangerously strengthened
by heavenly visions of unimpeachable orthodoxy. The Chamber,
however, was not impressed, and brought dissolution upon itself
in March 1830 by firmly demonstrating the lack of confidence with
which it viewed the Prince's administration. New elections in
July showed a further deterioration in the government's situation,
but the King was undismayed. The post-Restoration period had
been one of material progress and scientific advance. There was
intense literary and artistic activity, characterized by the
Romantic Movement of which Victor Hugo was the most celebrated protagonist. Overseas, substantial successes had been
gained. Had not a French naval contingent assisted the British and
Russians (all pledged to mediation) in blasting the Turkish fleet
out of the waters of Navarino Bay in aid of Greek Independence
(1827)? Had not a French force operated with success in the
Morea? Had not the pirate base of Algiers fallen to French arms
on 5 July 1830, starting a French military mystique comparable
with that which the Indian North-West Frontier was to offer the
British? Glory abroad seemed to justify resolute action at home,
expressed in Charles' "Four Ordinances of St. Cloud", announced
on 26 July. By these measures the press was effectively muzzled,
the new Chamber of Deputies dissolved without meeting, the
franchise restricted to a handful of landowners, and a day named
for fresh elections.

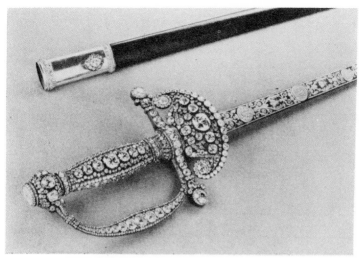

Diamond studded sword – made for the coronation
of Charles X by Frédéric Bapst
*(Louvre, Paris. Photo des Musées Nationaux)*

The barricades were swiftly up in Paris and there followed the
"Three Glorious Days" of 27, 28 and 29 July 1830. The Napoleonic turncoat Marmont, Duke of Ragusa, commanded the royal
troops, but, suffering under the summer sun from lack of food,
water and orders, evacuated the capital on the third day. It was
clear that the King must go. On 1 August he abdicated in favour
of the Duke of Bordeaux, his grandson, and left, with dignity, for
England. His departure, and that of the child designated as his heir,
opened the way for an Orleanist coup which brought to the throne
Louis Philippe, Duke of Orleans, son of the notorious Philippe
Egalité. Here was a direct descendant of the younger brother of
Louis XIV, an ex-member of the Jacobin Club, a veteran of Valmy
and Jemappes. A suitable blessing was readily available. The
septuagenarian La Fayette made a come-back with a charac-
teristic balcony scene. Before the Paris Hotel de Ville he was kissed
by the Duke, tricolour in hand, and, on 9 August 1830, the latter
acceded to the wish of the half-empty Chambers that he should
become Louis Philippe I, King of the French, a title evocative of
1789 and designed to emphasize the popular sanction of the new
July Monarchy.

Louis Philippe, by Any Scheffer 1795–1858
*( Musée Condé, Chantilly. Photo Giraudon)*

# LOUIS PHILIPPE, 1830–1848

(Son of Louis-Philippe-Joseph, Duke of Orleans – Égalité – and Louise-Marie-Adelaide of Bourbon-Penthièvre. Descended in direct line from Philip, Duke of Orleans, younger son of
## LOUIS XIII)

Born 1773, was 56 when he accepted the crown, and 74 when he abdicated.

Married Marie-Amélie of Bourbon-Sicily and had ten children. Of these the eldest son, Duke of Orleans, died in a carriage accident (1842). The loss of this popular heir jeopardized the dynasty. A daughter married Leopold, King of the Belgians; Clementine married Augustus of Saxe-Coburg-Gotha and became mother of Ferdinand of Bulgaria; the Duke of Montpensier married Maria Luisa of Spain.

*Thumbnail Sketch* Courageous, intelligent, well-educated and touchingly moral, "the bourgeois monarch of July is not so much a new nineteenth-century political portent as the last of the enlightened despots" (T. E. B. Howarth, *Citizen-King*). His weaknesses were "hesitancy in decision and a desire to be liked" (ibid.).

## WHAT TO KNOW

Louis Philippe was not unambitious and, if he had been asked to define the objects with which he accepted the crown, might have replied that he intended, personally, to drive the coach of state down a middle way between the principles of 1789 and those of the ancient monarchy. The bourgeois and pacific umbrella which, in the early days of his reign, he carried through the streets of Paris symbolizes the régime, frequent appearances on the balcony of the Palais Royal, ready to wave, and even to oblige with the "Marseillaise", betray his craving for popularity. France should be prosperous, contented and peaceful. Peace she had, except for continued and distinguished campaigning in Algeria – prosperity and contentment, like the extended suffrage, were by no means universal.

There was, in fact, built-in opposition to the Citizen-King. He did not represent the Republicanism of the July barricades, nor yet the Socialism expounded by Saint-Simon, Fourier and Louis Blanc. Similarly he was unacceptable to supporters of the elder Bourbon branch, while Bonapartist dissatisfaction grew as the Napoleonic Legend gained impetus, contrasting past glory with present boredom.

Disturbances were frequent during the first ten years of the reign. Mobs rioted in sympathy with rebellious Poles and insurgent Italians; unreasonable and abortive demands were made for the death of Charles X's ministers, Paris saw anti-clerical plundering and bloodshed in the streets; serious disorders were suppressed at Toulouse, Nîmes, Marseilles and, above all, Lyons – where the industrial revolution which France was undergoing produced characteristically deplorable workers' conditions; the Duchess of Berry raised the legitimist flag ineffectively in Vendée (1832); Louis Napoleon, nephew of the Emperor, made theatrical descents upon Strasbourg (1836) and Boulogne (1840), but had begun his six-year incarceration at Ham when his uncle's ashes, which he had intended to welcome, were borne amidst acclaim to the Invalides. Throughout all this the régime relied on the revived middle-class National Guard, whose support was to be sensationally withdrawn in 1848, while the King, under continual threat of assassination, faced attempts upon his life with courage and humour.

Foreign policy, with rare exceptions, showed a predictable bourgeois caution. The King, for instance, wisely refused the crown of newly constituted Belgium for his second son (1830), but married his eldest daughter to Leopold of Saxe-Coburg, by whom that crown was accepted. Thiers, on the other hand, by supporting the ambitious Mehemet Ali, Pasha of Egypt, courted the humiliation inflicted upon France by Palmerston, who considered the integrity of the Ottoman Empire to be menaced by the Porte's rebellious vassal ruler (1840). Finally Anglo-French relations were temporarily shattered when Guizot and his royal master engineered the Spanish

Sèvres Cup and Saucer
*(Collection Viollet)*

marriages of 1846; Queen Isabella of Spain with the Bourbon Duke of Cadiz, the Duke of Montpensier with the Queen's sister.

By 1848 many Frenchmen regarded their country's Foreign Policy as inept, while, at home, they resented the continued absence of franchise reform, were indignant about social conditions and hungry by reason of crop failures. Industrial development, railways, steam, better roads, brilliant literature and flourishing art – the happy achievements of the period – could not offset this. Liberal orators took to inflaming diners at political banquets, one of which, due to take place in Paris on 22 February, was forbidden by the authorities. Once again the barricades went up, Guizot fell, and, as it became clear that yet another revolution was in progress, Louis Philippe abdicated and made a furtive and perilous departure. On 3 March 1848 the ex-king and his consort, having temporarily assumed the unconvincing pseudonym of Mr. and Mrs. William Smith, stepped on to the quay at Newhaven and threw themselves upon the hospitable mercy of Queen Victoria.

Louis Napoleon, after Lafasse
*(Bibliothèque Nationale, Estampes, Paris)*

# SECOND REPUBLIC, 1848–1852

## WHAT TO KNOW

The "Citizen-King" had departed and a provisional government, dominated by a minority of socialists, took over. Its most interesting members were the historian and poet Lamartine, the advanced republican advocate Ledru-Rollin, the reformer Louis Blanc and, by reason of his being a workman, a certain Albert. Current problems were now attacked in idealistic fashion, with naïve faith in the possibility of a fresh start. Slavery came to an end in French colonies, execution for political crimes was abolished, and universal male suffrage was proclaimed. This momentous step created nine million voters who, by electing a National Constituent Assembly, in which Republicans and moderates formed the majority, proclaimed the fact that what Frenchmen really desired was order.

But order – particularly in Paris – was not easy to achieve. Dissatisfied persons listened eagerly to socialist orators and, by an abortive invasion of the Assembly on 15 May, demonstrated disapproval of that body's composition. Furthermore Louis Blanc's suggestion, under the Provisional Government, that the State should eradicate unemployment by directing labour, had resulted in the creation of over-subscribed and maladministered National Workshops, which put their clients to underpaid but expensive tasks of manifest fatuity. But even this seemed better than the alternative of abolition, with the precarious choices – clumsily offered – of private employment, work in the provinces or military service for the unmarried of the younger age-group. However the government closed the shops and the unemployed rose, with much of the working population of the capital in support. Dictatorial powers were then accorded to an honourable republican general – Cavaignac – who suppressed the insurrection during the bloody days 23–26 June 1848 with heavy casualties, which included the Archbishop of Paris.

"The Republic is dead", said Lamartine, as the constitution-makers started again. They provided for a President, elected by universal suffrage for four years (but not re-eligible without a four-year gap), and a Legislative Assembly, similarly chosen, which nominated a Council of State. Cavaignac, Ledru-Rollin and Lamartine were all candidates in the Presidential Election – but there sailed in the adventurer of Strasbourg and Boulogne, the prisoner of Ham – Louis Napoleon. Five major factors brought him to this office, and subsequently to the throne of the Second Empire: his supposed sympathy with the working-class, the overwhelming desire of Frenchmen for order, the unpopularity of Republicans as represented by "Butcher Cavaignac", the Royalist split between supporters of the Bourbons (Legitimists) and of the House of Orleans, and, above all, his great name, fostered and glorified by the now established Napoleonic Legend.

The Prince-President, knowing which way his star was leading, swiftly consolidated his position by cultivating Catholic opinion in France. Some months before its end (May 1849) the Constituent Assembly had approved a military expedition to Rome to defend Mazzini's republic, which had ejected Pius IX during the 1848 troubles, against possible Austrian intervention. But the faithful favoured the return of the Holy Father, and Louis Napoleon achieved this by a secret and fundamental change of the campaign's object. French troops remaining to protect Pius and the Patrimony of St. Peter until 1870. Similarly, on the domestic front, by the Loi Falloux of 1850, a private sector of education was permitted, which handed great influence to the religious orders.

Obvious and general popularity was achieved by well-staged tours and attractive speeches and, at certain military reviews, the gratifying cry of "Vive l'Empereur" was heard.

Indeed, in Louis Napoleon's opinion, the Republic had gone on long enough. The not easily managed Assembly disapproved suggestions that his civil list should be increased and his Presidency renewed without the constitutional four-year gap. He decided on a *coup d'état* – putting his faith in the invincible card represented by his hold over the army. On 2 December 1851 (Coronation Day Napoleon I, anniversary of Austerlitz) influential persons awoke to find themselves

Episode in the Revolution of 1848. "The
Password". Paris, 24 February 1848
*(Château of Versailles. Photo des Musées Nationaux)*

under arrest, Paris was placarded with decrees dissolving the
Chamber and restoring the universal suffrage which that body
had prejudiced by restricting the vote to citizens domiciled in
one place for three years – a blow at migratory workmen of
socialist views. There were prosecutions and deportations,
Victor Hugo went abroad and consoled himself by satirizing Louis
Napoleon in the "Châtiments", but a plebiscite overwhelmingly
approved the President's action, and confirmed him in office for
ten years. January 1852 saw a new constitution, almost identical
with that of the year VIII, which led, as had its predecessor, to
Empire – "*le Second Tant-pire*", as Léon Daudet called it. The
date was 2 December.

Napoleon III, by Noël, after Pierron
*(Bibliothèque Nationale, Estampes, Paris)*

# NAPOLEON III, 1852–1870

(Son of Louis Bonaparte, King of Holland, and Hortense de
  Beauharnais, nephew and step-grandson of NAPOLEON I)

Born 1808, was 44 when he became Emperor, 62 when the Empire
fell, and 64 when he died at Chislehurst.

Married Eugénie de Montijo, Countess of Teba, and had one son:
  Napoleon Eugène Louis – the Prince Imperial – killed in
  Zululand, 1879

*Thumbnail Sketch* A well-read, silent, conspiratorial adventurer
of marked distinction and courtesy. In character a curious mixture
of fatalist and opportunist, but with decided gifts in the social and
economic field.

## WHAT TO KNOW

Offenbach raises his baton, a diner orders ice-cream in the Café
de Paris and drops it into his boots, Lord Hertford (of London's
Wallace Collection) haunts the sale rooms, there is a mutter of
distant drums, and the curtain rises on the Second Empire. The
régime represents one of France's most colourful, if not most noble
periods, and was not barren of achievement when it stumbled to
its tragic fall.

Napoleon, despite his name (and authorship of a work on
artillery), was not a man of war. "The Empire means peace" he
declared in 1852, yet its army seldom lacked employment. The
desire for friendship with England, alarm at Russian ambition,
the urge to champion Catholic against Orthodox claims in Palestine's Holy Places, brought him into the Crimean War (1854–
1856). Sympathy with Italian aspirations for freedom and unity,
and a natural inclination to remove the motive of would-be
assassins like the nationalist Orsini, led him to help Piedmont in
the War of Italian Liberation (1859), emerging the richer by Nice
and Savoy. Outside Europe there was an ill-judged campaign in
Mexico (1861–1867) when England, Spain and France (creditors
of the defaulting President Juarez) tried to enforce their rights, and
the French stayed on, courting the Pope and the Hapsburgs, in an
abortive attempt to establish a Mexican Empire under an Austrian

Archduke. On the other side of the world French troops were active in China and Cochin-China (now South Vietnam) and, nearer home, in Syria.

But the arts of peace were also cultivated. Trade boomed, tariffs were lowered; agriculture, industry and communications developed vastly; much was achieved for public welfare; great material prosperity was demonstrated by the exhibitions of 1855 and 1867, while, under the supervision of the Prefect Haussmann, Paris – her bookstalls offering Baudelaire, Flaubert and Gautier, her salons gay with the paintings of the Impressionists – was transformed into the capital which few would deny to be the most enchanting in the world.

Nor did the Empire retain the dictatorial character of its start. The right – lay and clerical – was offended by the ruler's support of the anti-papal Cavour and disapproved the Free Trade movement, hence the trend had to lie in a liberal direction. So there was parliamentary revival, an unmuzzled press, freedom to form trades unions and to strike and, by 1869, virtually constitutional monarchy, with the Emperor retaining the typically Napoleonic right of direct appeal to his people by plebiscite.

But trouble was brewing beyond the Rhine. Prussia, under William I and Bismarck, had defeated Denmark in 1864, Austria in 1866 (while France was over-preoccupied

with Mexico) and now headed the North German Confederation. The final step to a united Germany, a consummation devoutly dreaded by French statesmen for centuries, could hardly be achieved without a Franco-Prussian showdown. And so it turned out. In 1868 a revolution drove Isabella II of Spain from her country. In July 1870 it became known that Prince Leopold of Hohenzollern-Sigmaringen was likely to accept the vacant throne. That France should view with distaste the prospect of a Hohenzollern ruler on her southern flank, as well as to the North-East, was understandable. Protests were made and Leopold stepped down, with the approval of his relative William I.

Reliquary diamond brooch made for the Empress Eugénie
*(Louvre, Paris. Photo des Musées Nationaux)*

Napoleon now pressed the Prussian King to promise that no member of his family would ever assume this office, an undertaking which William was not prepared to give. The account of the King's final – and courteous – interview with the French ambassador, as released to the press by Bismarck (Ems telegram), caused indignation on both sides of the Rhine and led to France's declaration of war on 17 July 1870 – an event for which both contestants bear responsibility – and which led, with incredible speed, to the Emperor's capitulation at Sedan on 1 September – triumph of Prussian staff duties and artillery superiority over French chaos and gallantry. A sinister precedent had been set for 1914 and 1940.

The Imperial magic, for some time diminishing, now departed. On 4 September 1870 the Third Republic was proclaimed.

Presidents Thiers, MacMahon, Grévy, Carnot, Casimir Périer,
Faure, Loubet, Fallières, Poincaré

*(Bibliothèque Nationale, Estampes, Paris)*

# THIRD REPUBLIC, 1870–1940
## Part 1, 1870–1914

Presidents: Thiers 1871, MacMahon 1873, Jules Grévy 1879, Sadi Carnot 1887, Casimir Périer 1894, Félix Faure 1895, Emile Loubet 1899, Armand Fallières 1906, Raymond Poincaré 1913

## WHAT TO KNOW

Harsh Prussian demands, secretly divulged, determined the Third Republic's provisional Government of National Defence to fight on, hopelessly, in view of lack of foreign support and of Marshal Bazaine's capitulation at Metz. The gallant minister of the interior, Gambetta, wafted by balloon from besieged Paris, could not stimulate a victorious provincial campaign. January 1871 saw William I declared German Emperor at Versailles. An armistice followed. A new Assembly, with a majority of Royalists (free of war blame) met at Bordeaux, and appointed Monsieur Thiers "Chief of the Executive of the French Republic". German regiments marched down the Champs-Elysées and peace terms – five milliards to pay, the cession of Alsace and Northern Lorraine – were accepted. On 18 March humiliated Paris established a traditional insurrectionary commune, bloodily suppressed by Marshal MacMahon, with a permanently divisive effect on French society. Peace was signed in May 1871 and the indemnity paid by 1873 – tribute to the economic miracle of the Second Empire and its successor. Royalists and Bonapartists now pushed Monsieur Thiers, "*libérateur du territoire*", into resignation, and the presidency went to MacMahon for seven years.

After the convulsions of 1787–1873 there was no realistic prospect of France's completing the nineteenth century (which ends logically in 1914) in political calm. It was assumed, by the powerful Right, that MacMahon's presidency portended Royalist Restoration, but the claimant, Charles X's grandson – the Count of Chambord – blind to the established glory of the tricolour, insisted unacceptably on the white flag of the Bourbons. 1875 saw a new constitution – with the mildly English flavour of a lower house (Chamber of Deputies), an upper house (Senate) and a non-responsible President. Symbolic of the period is the basilica of the Sacré-Coeur, started as an act of governmental piety in 1875, and completed in 1914 – by which time Church and State were separated. For this Republic, Conservative and Catholic at its inception, would be radical and anti-clerical when the century ended, never attracting the allegiance of all its subjects, and producing fifty prime ministers, often mediocrities, in less than that number of years.

Against this background scandals were to be expected. In 1887 President Grévy resigned on the revelation of his son-in-law's peculations over the Honours List. The malaise of 1889 might have upset the constitution to make General Boulanger head of state, but that egregious Celt fled in panic to Brussels. Nevertheless the centenary of the Great Revolution was celebrated with an Exhibition, the construction of the Eiffel Tower and an apolaustic repast for the country's mayors, jollifications marred by the crash of the Panama Company, with certain deputies discreditably involved. But the deepest shock was the Dreyfus Affair. It took from 1894 to 1906 to clear this Jewish officer of divulging secrets to Germany, and France split into Dreyfusards (Republicans, socialists, pacifists and anti-clericals) and anti-Dreyfusards (reactionary army aristocrats, anti-Semites and Catholics).

Gambetta's dictum: "Clericalism – there is the enemy" was adopted as policy. Jules Ferry (1882) secularized French primary education, now compulsory and free. Pope Leo XIII (1878–1903) strove to reconcile Church and Republic, but the century's turn saw teaching placed entirely in lay hands, the dissolution of many religious communities, and, in 1905, the separation of Church and State. Meanwhile French dynamism was demonstrated by growing industry, commerce, communications and finance; by developing trades unionism and socialism – while intellectuals and artists throve. *Littérateurs* progressively enjoyed Anatole France, Rimbaud and Péguy; galleries hung the Post-impressionists,

Triumphant Youth. (Rodin *c.* 1894)

*(William Morris Gallery, Walthamstow. Provisional gift of Frank Brangwyn 1940. Founder: Thiébaut Frères)*

Fauvists and Cubists; Pasteur and the Curies experimented, Bergson philosophized, César Franck gave new impetus to music, while theatre audiences were held spellbound by the Bernhardt.

Meanwhile, encouraged by Bismarck, France had been looking overseas rather than to the Rhine, and proconsuls, generals and missionaries had created the world's second greatest colonial Empire. German hopes that this would bring embroilment with Great Britain faded during Delcassé's brilliant Foreign Ministership (1898–1906). His fostering of the Franco-Russian alliance of 1892 and of the Entente Cordiale between France and England (1904) meant that, by 1907, a Triple Entente of France, Russia and Great Britain confronted the Triple Alliance of Germany, Austria-Hungary and Italy. The stage was being set for 1914.

# TWENTIETH CENTURY
## 1914–1984

| | |
|---|---|
| Third Republic | 1870–1940 |
| Part 2 1914 1940 | |
| Third Republic, | 1940–1944 |
| Part 3 and French State | |
| Provisional Government | 1944–1946 |
| Fourth Republic | 1947–1958 |
| Fifth Republic | 1958– |

*(In England)*

| | |
|---|---|
| George V | 1910–1936 |
| Edward VIII | 1936 |
| George VI | 1936–1952 |
| Elizabeth II | 1952– |

TWENTIETH CENTURY
*Pavillon Suisse*, Paris. (Le Corbusier 1929)

# TWENTIETH CENTURY
## 1914–1984

The twentieth century has witnessed architects of advanced views sometimes fighting an uphill battle against the forces of conservatism. One could almost have said, during the first four decades, that – amongst these architects – "concrete was King", instancing the Théâtre des Champs-Elysées (1913), Notre Dame du Raincy (1922) and the Mobilier National (1935), all the work of the brothers Perret. Auguste Perret was one of those who influenced Le Corbusier (1887–1965), whose expertise in painting and sculpture – matured by study in Austria and Germany – has made him the giant of the century. The *Pavillon Suisse* (concrete and steel frame) is the first great monument to his astonishing genius.

Research and building activity were firmly interrupted by World War II, while the concept of prefabrication was being developed in America. The immediate post-war construction in France was traditional (e.g. tufa and slate work in regional style at Tours), but, in about 1947, study began again and prefabrication was in. Economy meant austerity of style (with occasional "*baroque*" exceptions), while Le Corbusier battled against financial controls for his vision of *la ville radieuse*, realized in the *Unité de Marseille* (1946–1952). American influence has, naturally, been strong, and shows itself not only in advanced industrial architecture but also in dwellings, economically constructed, and infinitely more habitable than those achieved by traditional processes.

Architecture in France today exhibits two essentially healthy characteristics: co-operation between architects and contractors, and a desire to beat out coherent methods as a result of painstaking study and analysis.

Presidents Deschanel, Millerand, Doumergue, Doumer, Lebrun

*(Bibliothèque Nationale, Estampes, Paris)*

# THIRD REPUBLIC, 1870–1940
## Part 2, 1914–1940

Presidents: Raymond Poincaré 1913, Paul Deschanel 1920,
    Alexandre Millerand 1920, Gaston Doumergue 1924,
    Paul Doumer 1931, Albert Lebrun 1932

## WHAT TO KNOW

Europe in 1914 was not peaceful. Germany's volatile William II
was making a speciality of provocative gestures, war flickered in
the Balkans and, on 28 June 1914, the assassination of the heir to
the Austro-Hungarian Empire started a conflagration in which
France, Russia and Great Britain faced the central powers.

There followed four years from which France remembers, above
all, the miracle of the Marne, Verdun's horrific glory (under a
master of defence – named Pétain), the forward surge after
Ludendorff's final thrust, the enemy's submission in the railway
coach of the Supreme Allied Commander (Marshal Foch) at
Compiègne on 11 November 1918, mile upon mile of devastated
territory, and her one and a half million dead. "Never again",
Frenchmen said and, bitterly aware of the smallness of their
population as compared with that of Germany, attempted to
achieve a peace which would give them the security they craved.
Alsace and Lorraine came back, the Rhineland was to be permanently demilitarized and Germany disarmed. It also seemed
right to Europe's arbiters that the vanquished should admit their
war guilt, and (to the economically uninstructed) pay reparations
to restore the ravaged tracts of the Western Front. On 28 June 1919
the Hall of Mirrors at Versailles, in need of exorcism since the
Teutonic cheers of 18 January 1871, saw two dim German civilians
sign a treaty which did not fully satisfy French desires. "Tiger"
Clemenceau, her major war-winner, was held responsible and thus
failed to achieve the Republic's presidency when Poincaré's tenure
came to an end in 1920, while Marshal Foch, with cynical and
ghastly accuracy, stigmatized the settlement as "an armistice for
twenty years".

France (1919–1939) still presented the picture of political in-
coherence, industrial unrest, fiscal incompetence and military

unpreparedness associated with a Republic which could never command the allegiance of more than half its citizens, though this great country never lost the love of the civilized world. The right wing preponderance of the immediate post-war years was followed by a swing to the left, succeeded by a familiar kaleidoscope of governments in the 1930s. The Stavisky scandal of 1934, when a disreputable financier, likely to publicize corruption in high places, was thought to have died of a police-sponsored suicide, recalled the nineteenth century. In the last years before 1939 Communism was growing, the Royalist *Action Française* took on new life, while Fascist organizations like the *Croix de Feu* and the *Cagoulards* complicated the scene. Military thought, based on the Verdun defensive and the naïve hope – springing from that hideous slaughter – of a bloodless war, produced the Maginot Line of sophisticated fortifications, not planned to extend along the frontier with Belgium. It was hoped that the defence works and army of that country, a military ally of France since 1920, would cover this ugly 250-mile gap. Thus when, in 1936, Leopold III reverted to the neutral status proclaimed in 1839, France was faced with a critical problem. She made no real attempt to solve it. Nevertheless the country which, in nineteen years, produced Claudel, Gide, Proust, Valéry, Mistinguette and Le Corbusier;

where Mauriac, Cocteau, Montherlant and Malraux flourished; where Matisse illustrated Joyce's *Ulysses*; where one could laugh and cry over René Clair's films and be captivated by Maurice Chevalier – and where the art of living was understood as nowhere else, continued to offer a spiritual home to millions of Francophiles.

But grave danger loomed. The Treaty of Versailles had left Germany humiliated but heavily populated and potentially powerful, with France strong, though fearful for future security. Under Poincaré as Prime Minister the reparations pressure was kept up, notably by French occupa-

Glass Bowl. (Maurice Marinot 1934)
*(Victoria and Albert Museum. Crown Copyright)*

tion of the Ruhr in 1923 – but chauvinism gave way to the
internationalism of Briand, who dominated foreign relations
from 1925 to 1932. The Dawes Plan (1924) had rationalized
reparations, the Locarno Treaty (1925) and Kellogg Pact (1928)
gave illusory guarantees of European and world peace, the
Japanese invasion of Manchuria (1931) and Mussolini's Abys-
sinian adventure (1935) made mock of the League of Nation's
collective security, while, by 1933, the world economic crisis had
thrown up in Germany the foulest régime that modern history
has known. The new Führer, who had denounced the Versailles
*Diktat* for years, soon left the League, and France missed what
hindsight shows to have been a unique opportunity by her failure
to act in 1936, when Hitler reoccupied the demilitarized Rhineland with a mere three battalions. Thus the ill-judged policy of
appeasement, in which England and France shared, led, by way
of Austria and Czechoslovakia, to the opening of World War II
in 1939.

Philippe Pétain
*(Bibliothèque Nationale, Estampes, Paris)*

# THIRD REPUBLIC, 1870–1940

Part 3, 1939–1940

President: Albert Lebrun

and

# FRENCH STATE (ETAT FRANCAIS), 1940–1944

Chief of State: Philippe Pétain

## WHAT TO KNOW

Poland was crushed, Norway was invaded, a "phoney war" continued. Then, on 10 May 1940, into a France of which the morale was low, the leadership feeble and the strategy faulty, there swept the finest army the world had ever seen. France's continental allies capitulated, the British were bustled off her coasts, she herself fell. The armistice of 22 June 1940 was signed – in the railway coach of Marshal Foch at Compiègne.

And now a line was drawn running North-West from the general area of Geneva, turning West near Besançon, South near Tours and hitting the Pyrenees rather more than twenty miles from Biarritz – dividing the country into occupied and unoccupied France. The French submitted, perforce, to disarmament (except for an army of 100,000 men) but the Germans renounced any claim to their fleet. At Vichy, capital of unoccupied France, eighty-four-year-old Marshal Pétain initiated "The French State" (deemed "corporative" and dedicated to "Work, Family, Father-land") which attempted, with lapses into collaboration, to hold the enemy to his armistice promises – an attitude of apparent realism which is understandable, though, perhaps, not admirable. Meanwhile, outside Vichy France, the Germans exercised "the rights of an occupying power" and the depraved technicians of the Gestapo went about their obscene business. For a lift of the spirit the scene shifts to London and the activities of General de Gaulle.

This gallant, intelligent and determined officer had arrived on 17 June, in patriotic defiance of the tottering French government, to which Winston Churchill's proposal that "France and Great Britain shall no longer be two nations, but one Franco-British Union" seemed like "fusion with a corpse". On 18 June the

General, through the B.B.C., urged "all Frenchmen who still bear arms to continue the struggle". Thus the Free French Movement was born in the faith that France had lost "a battle, but not the war" But de Gaulle's path was hard. Britain was fighting for survival – a situation unconducive to charity amongst statesmen. President Roosevelt, to whom Churchill looked as leader of the ultimate intervention by the New World, distrusted the General from the start – attaching great importance to Vichy's retention of the French navy and control of the North African colonies. Yet the Battle of Britain presaged a long war, the Hitler-Pétain conversations at Montoire sickened many Frenchmen, and the closing year saw large areas of French Equatorial Africa rallying to the Cross of Lorraine. The winter of 1940 and spring of 1941 witnessed distinguished operations emanating from Chad, and also in Ethiopia, while, during the summer of the march on Moscow, a British-Australian-Free French force conquered Vichy-held Syria, which, due to de Gaulle's astute political initiative, passed under his control rather than that of the allies. In December 1941 de Gaulle further prejudiced his relations with America by seizing St. Pierre and Miquelon (off the St. Lawrence), though the courageous action at Bir Hakim (June 1942) won hearts both in Washington and London. The British-American descent upon North Africa in November 1942 was made without de Gaulle's knowledge, and the situation developed dramatically. The Germans marched into Vichy-France, the fleet at Toulon scuttled itself, and, in North Africa, the French forces, under command of ex-Vichy-ite minister Admiral Darlan, sided with the allies. But on 24 December Darlan was murdered and, as desired by the Americans, was succeeded by General Giraud, escaped prisoner of war, eleven years senior to de Gaulle. This excellent soldier was, however, no match politically for the leader of Free France, who had by now won the allegiance of the increasingly formidable resistance fighters in the home country, including the communists, highly active since Hitler's invasion of Russia. Nevertheless the two co-opera-

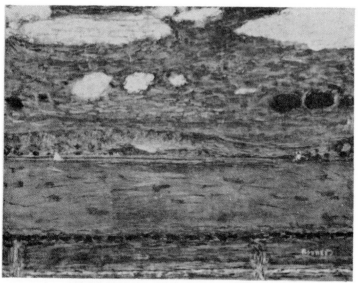

Mediterranean 1941–1944 (Pierre Bonnard)

ted over the French National Committee of Liberation (Algiers, 1943), a body which de Gaulle soon dominated and which, by April 1944, had manœuvred his rival into retirement. Backed by a Consultative Assembly, the Committee planned the post-invasion administration of France.

De Gaulle, ignorant of D-Day arrangements until 4 June 1944, sailed for France on 13 June and made a public appearance in Bayeux that afternoon. Immediately the Committee's planning began to pay off and, as the allies advanced, de Gaulle's highly prepared officials took over. The power of the French communists in Paris presented a major problem (a repetition of 1871 was extremely undesirable), but, after nine days of high adventure, de Gaulle entered the capital on 25 August and made it his own. The tide of battle swept on and Gaullist administration continued its triumph – substantiating the claim of the National Committee to be the provisional government of the country. In October 1944 recognition was achieved – America, Russia and Great Britain tardily acquiesced in what was, actually, a brilliant *fait accompli*.

Charles de Gaulle
*(Bibliothèque Nationale, Estampes, Paris)*

# PROVISIONAL GOVERNMENT, 1944–1946

President: Charles de Gaulle (until 20 January 1946)
Heads of Government: Félix Gouin, Georges Bidault

## WHAT TO KNOW

When the Provisional Government was recognized by the great powers on 23 October 1944, it had already been in existence for nearly eight weeks. The situation which it faced was, from every point of view, one of enormous difficulty. A hungry country, in all material ways impoverished, with its communications destroyed, its self-esteem deeply wounded and its regard for law and order severely impaired, was undergoing a physical and moral crisis. The occupation, during which the German regular forces, generally, behaved with conscientious correctness (though the Gestapo torture chambers were busy, and deportation created havoc) had posed agonizing problems. What did duty, or common sense, dictate? Collaboration, resistance or waiting upon events (*attentisme*)? All these alternatives found their followers, but it is significant that the intellectual giants of the period – the existentialist Jean-Paul Sartre and Albert Camus – both chose resistance, and it is interesting that the enemy authorities should have gone so far in their positive encouragement of the Paris theatre as to allow Anouilh's *Antigone* to pass their censorship. Anomaly was the order of the day.

Meanwhile hostilities continued and French armies fought with distinction – though the Supreme Allied Command frequently found General de Gaulle a thorn in the flesh. The new Head of State was preoccupied, above all, with the status of France as a power, and would, virtually, stick at nothing to ensure her alignment, on a basis of equality, with the United States, the U.S.S.R. and Great Britain. So orders were disregarded, and plans disrupted, as he manœuvred to this end. Nor was he unsuccessful. General Sevez was present at the German surrender in Rheims, General de Lattre de Tassigny (who had the satisfaction of provoking Keitel to explode with: "Frenchmen as well – that's the last straw!") in Berlin, while General Leclerc witnessed the capitulation of the Japanese in Tokyo Bay. In addition France had a zone of occupation in Germany and became a permanent member of the Security Council of the United Nations.

At home there was an unpleasant, but inevitable, period of revenge, in which numerous persons who had assisted the Germans, or who had fallen under suspicion of so doing, suffered. Marshal Pétain, removed by the Nazis to a gilded cage at Sigmaringen, and subsequently transferred to Switzerland, where he could have stayed, returned of his own volition in April 1945. Received by General Koenig – hero of Bir Hakim and co-ordinator of the Resistance – who rejected his proffered handshake, he was put on trial. The old gentleman, who had cast himself, no doubt sincerely, as France's buckler rather than France's sword, had clearly become, since 1942, increasingly tarred with the collaborationist brush, wielded by Laval. In August 1945 sentence of death was passed upon him, immediately commuted to life imprisonment. He died on 23 July 1951, aged ninety-five, on the Vendéan Île d'Yeu, where he lies buried. With the passage of time it may be that charity will overcome other emotions and see in Verdun's Douaumont Cemetery his proper resting place.

In all her history France had never been in such tragic need of rehabilitation, and, as a result of able administration and American aid, recovery was achieved with astonishing speed. Civil Service training was vastly improved and de Gaulle laid emphasis on

Flight into Egypt. (Georges Rouault) 1946

*( Musée National d'Art Moderne.* © *by S.P.A.D.E.M. Paris 1970. Photo des Musées Nationaux)*

maintaining a large, well-equipped army – incurring unpopularity by readiness to employ men who had served Vichy and as the result of a widely held feeling that he was more interested in power than in welfare.

The elections of October 1945 (now and henceforth women voted) showed an overwhelming desire for a new constitution and charged ɾ Constituent Assembly to create it. But this object had not been achieved when, in January 1946, de Gaulle, disagreeing with the Assembly over military estimates, resigned the Presidency conferred upon him two months previously. Félix Gouin, the socialist leader, carried on, with a ministry combining his own party, Christian Democrats (Mouvement Républicain Populaire) and communists. After an abortive attempt to satisfy the country with the constitution of May 1946, Georges Bidault took over and another Constituent Assembly designed a Fourth Republic: President, Council of the Republic and National Assembly. A lethargic referendum brought acceptance of these arrangements by a narrow majority.

President Vincent Auriol
*(By permission of Radio Times Hulton Picture Library)*

President Coty
with Queen Elizabeth II during her visit to France, Spring 1957
*(By permission of Radio Times Hulton Picture Library)*

# FOURTH REPUBLIC, 1947-1958

Presidents: Vincent Auriol 1947, René Coty 1954

## WHAT TO KNOW

After all that France had suffered it is hardly surprising that the period of the Fourth Republic should be one beset with difficulties. Communists, socialists, radicals, the moderate "Mouvement Républicain Populaire" (M.R.P.) and de Gaulle's "Rassemblement du Peuple Français" (R.P.F.) jostled upon the political stage with the familiar instability of changing coalitions. There was industrial and social unrest at home despite which, under the Monnet plan and with Marshall aid, an astonishing work of modernization and reconstruction went forward. Intellectual life was vivid. Three French authors – André Gide, François Mauriac and Albert Camus – won the Nobel Literature prize in 1947, 1952 and 1957 respectively. Classics, existentialists, exponents of the "new novel" and of the "new drama" were active. A guilt-ridden *avant-garde* theatre made its appearance with the works of the Rumanian Eugène Ionesco ("The Bald Prima Donna", 1950) and the Irishman Samuel Beckett ("Waiting for Godot", 1953). Both these dramatists have been honoured subsequently – Ionesco recently joined the immortals of the French Academy and Beckett the Nobel Prize winners.

In 1949 France took her place in NATO and, during the premiership of Robert Schuman (1947-1948) the remarkable economist Jean Monnet suggested a plan which led, in 1951, to the creation of the European Coal and Steel Community, of which the members are the Netherlands, Belgium, Luxembourg, France, West Germany and Italy. This initiative was followed, in 1957, by the Treaty of Rome – when the same nations added the European Economic Community (the Common Market) and the European Atomic Energy Committee (Euratom) to the already established E.C.S.C. Here were steps towards political union in which some see Europe's salvation, though in 1955 the French Assembly had found the conception of a European Defence Community too great a sacrifice to supra-nationalism.

All this was played against a background of virtually ceaseless military operations. Indo-China – consisting of Tongking, Annam, Cochin-China, Cambodia and Laos – had come under French sway between 1862 and 1904. In 1941 this area fell to the Japanese and, on their defeat, inherited the familiar legacy of nationalism and communism – represented by the party called Vietminh. Under Ho Chi Minh this organization fought the French from 1946 to 1954, when the latter suffered the decisive disaster of Dien Bien Phu. Thereafter agreements at Geneva metamorphosed Tongking, Annam and Cochin-China into Northern and Southern Vietnam, flanked by the Kingdoms of Cambodia and Laos. In their newly found independence the three last-named sought their security from America rather than as members of the French Union – the former French Empire had borne this title since 1944. Indeed change of nomenclature had failed to bring solidarity, and this was soon observed elsewhere. Troubles in Morocco, scene of the triumphs of Marshal Lyautey before and during the First World War, led to independence in 1955. Tunisia went the same way a year later. But it was the Algerian crisis which toppled the Fourth Republic.

The French army had had its first major post-Napoleonic success in that country in 1830, deriving therefrom a military mystique of which mention has already been made (see page 196). Here also well-established colonists had laboured for generations, and here, in 1954, members of the Front de Libération Nationale (F.L.N., National Liberation Front) started their battle for independence which was to last until 1961. In the course of four troubled war years, which included French participation (with Great Britain and Israel) in the controversial Suez operation of 1956, governmental instability and crises were such that, on 29 May 1958, President Coty saw no alternative but to seek a saviour for France by asking General de Gaulle to form a government once more. The sixty-seven-year-old General was ready and willing to undertake this task.

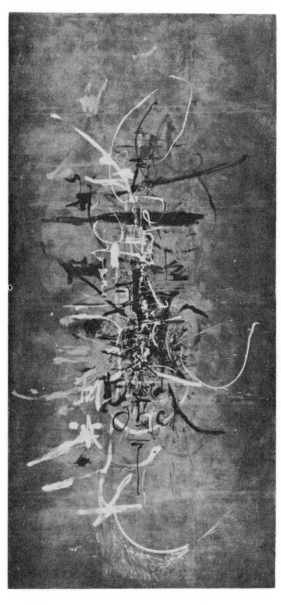

Les Capetiens partout. (Georges Mathieu) 1954

*(Musée National d'Art Moderne. By courtesy of Monsieur Georges Mathieu. Photo des Musées Nationaux)*

This picture bears no relation to historical events

General de Gaulle, President of the Republic
*(Photo Marcel Viollet)*

# FIFTH REPUBLIC, 1958–(1984)

Presidents: Charles de Gaulle 1958, Georges Pompidou 1969, Valéry Giscard d'Estaing 1974, François Mitterrand 1981

## WHAT TO KNOW

The first problem which faced "the most illustrious of Frenchmen", as Coty had called de Gaulle, was that of authority. To achieve his object he needed full powers, and he got them. On 21 December 1958 he became President of the Fifth French Republic which, by then, had existed for some eleven weeks. Despite certain crises the new constitution, with its great increase in Presidential control, gave French politics a degree of stability unknown since 1870.

The General immediately turned his attention to Algeria, where, as he clearly saw, the only realistic solution lay in the grant of independence. As he moved in this direction he incurred the passionate enmity first of the colonists and secondly of a powerful group of army officers – both civilians and soldiers having originally expected him to back their concept of "Algérie française". This brought the country to the verge of civil war and exposed the Head of State to grave danger of death by assassination over a period of two years. He however, with massive popular backing, directed his efforts majestically and courageously to the end which he had appointed. It came on 4 July 1962, from which day the Republic of Algeria has been in existence.

It is impossible to consider this – the final de Gaulle period – without placing major emphasis on his foreign policy, an emphasis which does not imply that he neglected the domestic front or that there was no domestic progress in France. Indeed the President long retained the affectionate respect of his country, helped by an elaborate technique of carefully planned provincial tours and brilliantly directed television appearances. His command of mass communication no doubt exercised influence on the referendum of 1962, which approved an amendment to the constitution whereby, in future, the election of the President of the French Republic was to be determined (in the tradition of Louis Napoleon) by universal suffrage.

In his foreign policy de Gaulle's object is easily discernible. It was to restore and maintain the traditional greatness of his country and achieve her position as leader of Europe, poised between the colossal powers of the United States on the one hand and the Soviet Union on the other. But though he could envisage a block of allied European nations, he rejected emphatically the supra-nationalism implicit in the idea of the Common Market. The desire to dominate was expressed in his determination that France should become a nuclear power – a goal attained by the Sahara explosion of 1960. There followed the wooing of Western Germany and – logically, if unfortunately – consistent opposition to Britain's "entry into Europe", hostility to NATO (with its American Supreme Commander) from which France had dissociated herself by 1967, and continual attacks upon the U.S.A., offset by a courting of the Kremlin, which received a dusty answer in the Czechoslovak tragedy of 1968. Indeed, as time went on, the General's foreign political pronouncements became increasingly didactic and provocative, until there was no power likely to escape, for long, his gratuitous advice or lofty rebuke.

Perhaps the French themselves became fatigued by the theatricality with which the nation had had thrust upon it the role of the pre-1914 Great Sovereign State, and, despite educational, industrial, social, fiscal and judicial reform, despite technological

advance, there were elements which wearied of Gaullist benevolent despotism. Student unrest, of which the complicated origins may eventually be traced to California or China (though the grievances of the French universities were probably more real than those obtaining in any other country), was typical of a generation in no way predisposed to pious contemplation of tradition, however glorious. The famous march from Nanterre to Paris (2 May 1968), under an international figure called Cohn-Bendit, resulted in the calling out of riot police, which immediately inspired large numbers of the industrial proletariat to join the students in a unique alliance against the establishment.

Memorial to the Martyrs of the Deportation

*(Illustration from the brochure: "Mémorial des Martyrs de la Déportation", produced by the "Réseau du Souvenir" with the support of the "Ministère des Anciens Combattants" and the "Commissariat Général du Tourisme")*

A welter of discontents – to do with overcrowding, academic methods, expensive nuclear armaments and authoritarianism – brought thousands to the barricades, but, after inexplicable hesitations during a visit to Rumania, the indefatigable President, sure of the army, overcame the crisis and, a few weeks later, triumphed at the polls. But it was not to be for long. In reality many Frenchmen were disenchanted by arbitrariness and an opportunity to express this sentiment was provided by the referendum of 27 April 1969 – as the result of which Charles de Gaulle at last announced his intention of ceasing to exercise the functions of his high office.

And so an age passed – ending with the great question mark scrawled upon the page of history by the events of May 1968. There can be little doubt that Gaullist methods are now anachronistic, yet few will deny that the protagonist of these methods gave his country "quelques années de grandeur".

President Pompidou being welcomed by Edward Heath at
Northolt Airport, 17 March 1972
*(Photo BBC Hulton Picture Library)*

President Giscard d'Estaing
*(Photo Camera Press, London)*

President Mitterrand
*(Photo Gisèle Freund,
by permission of the
French Embassy, London)*

The Pompidou Centre in Paris, seen from the piazza
*(French Government Tourist Office. Photo François Darras)*

Since the resignation of de Gaulle there have been three Presidents: Georges Pompidou (1969-1974), a Gaullist, whose memory is enshrined in the great Centre in Paris which bears his name, and whose close connections with Edward Heath resulted in the United Kingdom's joining the Common Market in 1973; Valéry Giscard d'Estaing (1974-1981), right-wing but not a Gaullist, now trying to popularize his essentially aristocratic image; and, since 1981, François Mitterrand, a socialist, whose efforts have won, oddly enough, a measure of Right and Gaullist praise and some sharp criticism from the extreme Socialist Left.

Mitterrand's rash promise of a dramatic reduction in unemployment remains unfulfilled, and the Communists (no longer participating in the government) now adopt the traditional pessimism of ancestral voices prophesying social and economic disaster. The project of abolishing Catholic private schools, dear to left-wing anti-clericals, has been abandoned; and the previous policy of economic growth, based on a Keynesian stimulation of consumption, has been replaced by a tough deflationary rigour. Laurent Fabius, the present Prime Minister, is a highly educated "republican élitist" and pragmatist, whom the Press has already referred to as "the New Dauphin".

In recent years France has become a strong supporting member of NATO (albeit not represented on its military committee), a firm advocate of the American missile deployment policy in Europe, and a nuclear power in her own right. With a population of a little over 54 million inhabiting an area of 213,000 square miles (compare the United Kingdom cramming its $55\frac{3}{4}$ million into less than half the French living space), France continues to enjoy the taste of renewed greatness which de Gaulle gave her, and once more plays a proud and purposeful role in European and world affairs.

# INDEX

Ronald Hamilton
*A Holiday History of France*

'If it finds its place in your rucksack or car, if it lies on your table between your *Guide Michelin* and a refreshing carafe. . . if it makes your French holiday more enjoyable, then it will have fulfilled its purpose.'

Making the past both informative and fun, Ronald Hamilton gives us a succinct and coherent guide to French history – from the Capet kings to President Mitterrand. His character sketches, the short accounts of each reign, and many illustrations showing the styles of the time, bring the country's rich heritage vividly to life. Witty and learned, this book is the perfect partner for all those who set off, briskly or gently, to explore the glories of France.

# M. F. K. Fisher
## *Two Towns in Provence*

Over the years, M. F. K. Fisher, widely regarded as one of America's finest contemporary writers and most highly esteemed of all authorities on the pleasures of the table, has spent much of her time living and travelling round France. Here she celebrates, in her uniquely perceptive, evocative fashion, Aix-en-Provence and Marseilles. Weaving together topography, history, folklore and personal memoirs with the look, the sound, the smell and (above all, perhaps) the taste of her chosen cities, M. F. K. Fisher provides the traveller, the gourmet and the lover of France and fine writing with unforgettable portraits of two remarkable and highly individual towns.